'*Detox Your Culture* is for any leader who wants to build a high-performing team. This book highlights the importance of the workplace culture.'

Tim Cahill AO, Technical Director, Qatar FA &
Chief Sports Officer, Aspire Academy

'This fascinating and easy-to-read book is a must-have for all HR and people managers who need their workforces to survive and thrive in the modern corporate world. It is full of practical insights and tips for achieving a healthy workplace culture along with thought-provoking real-life case studies.'

Paul O'Halloran, Partner, Dentons Australia

'This book is a "must-read" for anyone who cares about culture and the impact it has on them, their colleagues, and the industry in which they work. It is a perfect read for anybody that wants their team or business to thrive.

'The real-life examples, from Colin's outstanding research and his own experiences, allow the reader to benchmark their experiences, both positive and negative. This book does a great job of holding a mirror up to the reader and allows us to investigate how we have contributed to the culture of the organizations to which we have belonged.'

David Moore, Head of Programs, Bangladesh Cricket Board

'Colin is simply your essential guide through the complexities of today's workplace. Culture isn't hard, but navigating modern issues is. This handbook is a must-have for all leaders everywhere, new and experienced alike.'

Deb Cramb, Senior leader VFX / Animation Industry

'Ellis pulls off the difficult trick of combining vivid case studies and examples of toxic cultures whilst providing a pragmatic and useful guide to improvement. For leaders and professionals in organizations large or small, if you care about your culture this book should be required reading.'

David D'Souza, Director of Profession, CIPD

'Colin Ellis reminds us that we all play a part in our workplace culture, for better and for worse. His insights into toxic culture, its causes and its remedies, have never been more important. If someone has left this on your desk with a Post-it note attached, read it immediately.'

Alex Cramb, Public Relations and Communications Expert

'*Detox Your Culture* is like a kale smoothie for your workplace. Blend toxic behaviours, a splash of passive-aggressiveness, and outdated policies. Voilà! A recipe for disaster. Grab a copy, purge those vibes, and brew a well-organized Earl Grey culture.'

Clare Brown, Director, Microsoft

'At last – a guide that arms readers with actionable strategies to confront and overcome the pervasive issue of toxic culture. Every senior manager should read this book.'

The European

'Toxic culture in the workplace doesn't just impact bosses – it harms everyone. This book provides the actions required to deal with toxicity before it poisons your business.'

Chris Riches, Correspondent for North-West England and Wales, Daily Express

'Punchy, practical and pragmatic. Ellis once again hits you with the facts about how even vibrant strategies can turn toxic if you're not paying attention. He backs it up by providing practical steps any leader can take to keep your team, function or company on the path to success.'

Alicia Aitken, GM Investment Delivery & Change, ANZ Bank

DETOX
YOUR
CULTURE

Deliver results, retain staff, and strengthen your organization's reputation

Colin D. Ellis

BLOOMSBURY BUSINESS
LONDON • OXFORD • NEW YORK • NEW DELHI • SYDNEY

BLOOMSBURY BUSINESS
Bloomsbury Publishing Plc
50 Bedford Square, London, WC1B 3DP, UK
29 Earlsfort Terrace, Dublin 2, Ireland

BLOOMSBURY, BLOOMSBURY BUSINESS and the Diana logo are trademarks of
Bloomsbury Publishing Plc

First published in Great Britain 2024

A catalogue record for this book is available from the British Library

Library of Congress Cataloguing-in-Publication data has been applied for

ISBN: 978-1-3994-1407-4; eBook: 978-1-3994-1409-8

2 4 6 8 10 9 7 5 3 1

Typeset by Deanta Global Publishing Services, Chennai, India
Printed and bound in Great Britain by CPI Group (UK) Ltd, Croydon CR0 4YY

To find out more about our authors and books visit www.bloomsbury.com and sign up
for our newsletters

This book is dedicated to anyone who has suffered physically or emotionally in their place of work. My aim with this book is to not only bring awareness to the issues that people face every day when trying to earn a living, but also to provide the information on how to change these conditions so that people can flourish in whatever they choose to do.

'If you don't start from a position of fear, you're probably not paying attention.'

Mustafa Suleyman, Artificial Intelligence Researcher and Entrepreneur[1]

Contents

Introduction: Why should you care?

'You can prove anything with facts.'
Stewart Lee, comedian

In picking up this book, you might be thinking, 'Why should I read a business book about culture, isn't that for my boss to do?' It's a fair question, so I thought I'd start with some facts about toxic culture, not least that it can be created by anyone and it can affect everyone:

- One in four people dreads going to work[1]
- People with high levels of work stress were 22 times more prone to suicidal thoughts[2]
- Employee turnover triggered by toxic culture costs US employers alone nearly $50bn each year[3]
- Culture is 12.4 times more likely than compensation to predict whether an employee leaves[4]
- Middle managers are 2.5 times more important in predicting employee misconduct compared to company-wide factors[5]
- One in five people have left their job due to culture[6]
- Bullying and harassment are systemic in many organizations[7]
- Odds of suffering a major disease increase by 35–55 per cent[8]
- Fifty-three per cent of women were more likely to experience toxic culture than men[9]
- The creators of toxic culture are often known serial offenders, yet not dealt with[10]

- Extremely disengaged employees are 20 per cent less productive than their engaged counterparts[11]
- Toxic culture can lead to employee suicide[12]
- Toxic social norms increase the chances that even good people start to behave poorly.[13]

All of these facts relate to the lived experience of employees within a toxic culture and it's far more prevalent than you might think. Indeed, in a poll I ran on LinkedIn while finalizing this chapter, I asked a simple question, 'Have you ever worked in a culture that you considered to be toxic?' Ninety-five per cent of people said that they had, which is an incredibly high number.

Every single member of every team, in every company, in every sector, in every country in the world, needs to be able to recognize the signs of toxic culture and understand the actions required to deal with it. Better still would be to create the conditions where toxic culture doesn't arise in the first place.

This book will hopefully save your mental health, physical health, career, company, reputation or all of these things. Toxic culture doesn't go away over time. Ignoring it won't make it magically disappear and bringing in consultants to 'conduct a process' over too long a time period to tell you what you already know also won't work. Toxic culture needs to be dealt with, and it needs to be dealt with now. This book will show you how your culture can turn toxic and, if it does, it will show you how you can recognize it, address it and defeat it.

CHAPTER ONE

What is toxic culture?

'I'll tell you what's toxic and I've always found it
toxic, aubergine. Do you like aubergine? Do you?
Do you like aubergine because I don't like aubergine?
It's just a personal thing.'

*TV Editor Martin Frizzell, when asked
whether his TV show had a toxic culture*[1]

For the benefit of clarity, a person can consider a culture to be toxic if
they witness or are subject to, one or more of the following elements:

- Bullying
- Harassment
- Racism
- Sexism
- Misogyny
- Misandry
- Homophobia
- Age-ism
- Unwanted physical contact
- Verbal or emotional abuse
- Lack of workforce diversity
- Non-inclusive
- A lack of trust
- Poor communication
- Hubris

- Unrealistic targets
- Unclear expectations
- Inequity of pay
- Inequity of conditions
- Fear
- Favouritism
- Blame
- Criticism
- Poor work/life balance
- Exclusion
- Injustice
- Avoidance of accountability
- The requirement to be continuously positive
- Malicious gossip
- Unethical behaviour
- Abuse of power
- Excessive workload
- Abuse of productive time
- Actions that betray company purpose and values.

And in reference to the quote that opened this chapter:

- An unwillingness to address concerns that staff may have; and
- poor communication.

In May 2023, Martin Frizzell, editor at ITV's *This Morning*, was doorstepped by the media to get his insights into the allegations that the show for which he is editor had a toxic culture. This followed the high-profile departure of star presenter Phillip Schofield (and subsequent admissions that he'd had an 'unwise, but not illegal affair' with a staff member, which seemingly lots of people knew about but no one talked about). In his press statement on the reasons for his resignation, Schofield said, 'In all the years I worked there, there was no toxicity.'[2] Which might have been true… for him. His co-presenter Holly Willoughby, however, felt differently, saying on Instagram that she'd asked Schofield whether the rumours were true and he'd said not and that, 'It's been very hurtful to now find out that this was a lie.'[3]

Others went public with their allegations of a toxic culture, which led to the doorstepping of Frizzell. Rather than just keeping quiet, he answered obtusely and somewhat arrogantly and brought further media coverage to bear. He also said that 'scores are being settled' in relation to the allegations of toxicity and told reporters to 'read between the lines'.[4]

Group Director of Strategy, Policy and Regulation at ITV Magnus Brooke, when grilled about Frizzell's response by the UK government Culture, Media and Sport Committee shortly afterwards, said that it was 'extremely ill-judged to say what he did'. He continued: 'I can reassure you on behalf of ITV that we do take all of these allegations very seriously, precisely because we do have a culture where people's conduct matters enormously.'

But the damage was already done and a difficult situation had been compounded even further. ITV Chief Executive Dame Carolyn McCall wrote to UK Culture Secretary Lucy Frazer, Chair of the Digital, Culture, Media and Sport committee, Dame Caroline Dinenage, and the Ofcom Chief Executive, Dame Melanie Dawes, to provide them with reassurance that they were taking the allegations seriously. In the letter she said, 'We are fully committed to providing every opportunity for anyone who works with us to raise any concern or comments they may have…we appointed an external and independent adviser to carry out a review. This external review found no evidence of bullying or discrimination.'[5]

What's interesting here is what one person considers to be a toxic culture is another person's vibrant culture. That's because what people perceive to *be* toxic can be quite different. This needs to be borne in mind and I will talk about scurrilous claims of toxic culture in Chapter 10: How will you respond? However, if just one person raises any one of these issues then that's enough for a full investigation to be considered. As you'll see, often the culture isn't 'safe' enough for people to feel that they can report issues and that seems to have been the case with ITV.

Just three weeks after receiving the letter, Dame Caroline Dinenage responded, saying that rejecting a toxic culture exists was incorrect. She said, '[Employees] speak with great pride about working at ITV and are hugely positive about many of their colleagues. However, they also raise claims of toxic working cultures, bullying, discrimination and harassment.'

The view of what's acceptable and what's not in the workplace has rightly changed. Most employees are better at judging what is appropriate and reasonable and are much better at assessing the level of humanity that is brought to bear in each situation. People aren't unnecessarily dragged out of their comfort zones, publicly humiliated or shamed based on weight, looks, gender, knowledge or race. Well, most people aren't. Incredibly, there are still some who don't understand what *is* right or wrong. There are still people who force employees into situations that they don't want to be in or use inappropriate language. Indeed, I was watching a football manager being interviewed yesterday and he talked about 'always getting told off for the things I say'. It's my view that it is incumbent on him to learn and be better.

I talk more about these people and their behaviours in Chapter 9: Are you standing still? However, it's still worth asking the following question for you to consider as you read this book…

Are you the problem?

I'm not saying you *are* the problem – and if you lack self-awareness then you definitely won't be – but it's worth continually asking yourself this question while reading this book. You have to be prepared for the fact that you could, at the very least, be contributing to a degradation of working conditions. Especially if you're part of a leadership team of a company in the midst of a toxic culture crisis.

Before you commission an expensive review, you could save some time and money by asking yourselves – as the comedy double act Mitchell and Webb did in a sketch when dressed as Nazis with skulls on their caps – 'Are we the baddies?'[6] Now, of course, I'm not saying that toxicity comes from thinking or dressing like a Nazi but some people in a work context have managed to draw the media's attention to their culture by doing just that.

Dressing up as Nazi officers is exactly what happened at a Colombian police academy[7] during a – wait for it – 'cultural event'. The incident drew widespread anger, condemnation and led to greater scrutiny of the force as a whole. Indeed, the country's president announced two months later that he was completely overhauling the police force as a result.[8] Not one of the leaders in that organization thought to send those officers home at the time, make a statement condemning their actions or to apologize retrospectively for their insensitivity, so all were culpable and therefore they were the 'baddies' in this scenario.

On the face of it, it's easy to say 'what the hell were they thinking?' and yet, this question can be applied to almost every toxic culture story that you read in this book and many of those that appear in the news every day. The simple fact is that, more often than not, people aren't thinking. Which is why your behaviour, lack of understanding of how humans work together today or what's appropriate and what's not could be a key contributor to the toxic culture that you are presiding over or indeed are part of. At the very least you're expected to be a good human being, to stay in touch with the world and positively contribute not only to those around you, but the culture of the organization itself. Of course you can't be perfect and you're going to make the odd mistake or two, but at the very least you could:

- Be polite
- Smile once in a while
- Be present
- Show an interest in others

- Find ways to contribute
- Perform a random act of kindness every now and again
- Say good morning or good night
- Elevate others
- Be welcoming
- Be willing to consider the views of others.

Every human is just trying to do their best every day with what they've been given. Almost no one wants to come to the office to be the worst version of themselves, but some days definitely require more work than others.

Now I don't want to point the finger too early; I'm just saying that it's possible, particularly if you've been given this book as a 'gift', it has mysteriously appeared on your desk with a Post-it note that says 'We thought you'd enjoy this', or it's signed with the note, 'Read this before you do anything else.'

If you come to the realization at any stage while reading this book that you are the problem, then you need to take immediate action. Do not ignore it and hope it goes away – it most definitely won't.

Toxic culture is everywhere

When it comes to toxic culture, most employees are usually not the problem, they are usually on the receiving end of toxic culture, however. This is still very hard for many people in senior positions to believe, but feedback on just one of the elements listed at the start of this chapter – when proven – is enough to bring unwanted scrutiny to the organization.

Just like those who provided feedback as part of a review into the working conditions at The University of Prince Edward Island in Canada. One person said, 'UPEI is the most miserable, soul-sucking place of work I have ever experienced.'[9] A pretty damning indictment, but as you'll read, the consequences of toxic culture can have far more disastrous consequences that people will never, ever forget. Indeed, toxic culture is far more prevalent than you think and has the potential to affect almost every business of every size in every country of the world.

In recent years organizations such as Uber,[10] Amazon,[11] Ubisoft,[12] BuzzFeed,[13] the Canadian rowing team,[14] Australia's Antarctic base,[15] ActivisionBlizzard[16] and even *The Ellen Show*[17] (to name but a small few that aren't the British Royal Family) have all faced allegations of toxic culture in the news. Those on the receiving end of toxic behaviour have suffered emotional and physical pain and the companies themselves have suffered reputational damage and loss.

Regardless of whether you've been on the receiving end of toxic culture for a sustained period of time, experienced it for an hour, or don't really know what it is/haven't experienced it before (lucky you!), it's crucial that you know how to spot it and call it out and also that you know what to do to ensure that one isn't created on your watch.

There is never any excuse for a toxic culture, yet many people continue to try and explain it away in the hope of avoiding any consequences. In my work, I have heard most of the excuses and none of them are justifiable. Some of those excuses include:

- 'Stress levels were high'
- 'You don't understand [name of person], that's who they are'
- 'We were under pressure to deliver'
- 'We had stretch targets to hit'
- 'They didn't complain about it at the time'
- 'People just need to get on with it'
- 'If you can't stand the heat, get out of the kitchen'
- 'All this fluffy stuff gets in the way of work'
- 'People are easily offended these days'
- 'If I didn't lose my temper, nothing would get done'
- 'Timescales are tight, risks need to be taken'

- 'We don't have time for breaks'
- 'Diversity and inclusion is the latest HR fad'
- 'People respond to swearing'
- 'If you're going to drink with the big boys, you have to face the consequences'
- Or, as Luis Rubiales, former head of the Spanish Football Federation said (more about him later), 'It's just a witch-hunt by false feminists.'[18]

Are any of these familiar to you? These are all excuses that bad managers or employees often make for cultivating or enabling an environment that causes stress, anxiety, fear and at its worse, depression and/or suicide.[19]

Some senior business managers may scoff at these consequences for an unhealthy workplace and blame other factors. More often than not, the reviews that they commission simply tell them what employees have been telling them already or else they outline the basics required for creating a vibrant culture, that an HR or people and culture manager, should really know how to do. As an example, one company had a member of staff commit suicide as a result of persistent bullying behaviour. This despite the fact that the person in question – and others around them – had reported to his company that they were the 'victim of sustained, unresolved workplace bullying'. They were working 16-hour days and received no support from management, leading to a sense of hopelessness and isolation. Not long afterwards, they took their life.[20]

Unfortunately, these kinds of cases are not isolated and occur almost everywhere. According to one survey, approximately one in 10 workers experience a toxic workplace.[21] At time of writing, levels of workplace stress and anxiety are at an all-time high.[22]

Not only do toxic cultures harm individuals, they also harm business performance. This cost is estimated to be as high as US$223bn over a five-year period.[23] Targets or deadlines are routinely missed, decisions are avoided, there is more work than the company and its employees have the time for, unproductive or confusing activities dominate working days and people behave poorly towards each other, leading to active detachment.

And when employees feel emotionally detached at work (regardless of where they may be doing it), it undermines their confidence, productivity and willingness to participate in activity which may help to address the reasons why the culture is toxic in the first place. The phrase 'people don't leave jobs, they leave bosses' might satisfy the need for blame, however, the kind of culture a person works in is 12 times more likely to predict whether someone leaves or not.[24]

Stories around toxic cultures used to centre on office-based, corporate entities. However, that situation has changed and incorporates all kinds of companies across a range of sectors and industries. Sports (even my own sports team!),[25] transportation, retail and the entertainment industry have all been in the media in recent years. Toxic cultures are everywhere and exposure of them is becoming more widespread.

Websites such as Glassdoor (*see also* p. 172) now allow employees to shine a light on toxic cultures (see Chapter 10: How will you respond?). Where people believe that their feedback isn't being listened to, they are using technology and social media to tell the world and the media have started to (sometimes justifiably) feast on these stories for weeks and months on end until meaningful action is taken.

These avoidable scenarios are playing out around the world and senior managers have a chance to intervene and address the issues to prevent them becoming public. As soon as a company and its culture find its way into the media, they will find it harder to retain and recruit the people they need to get them out of the mess that they're in. These stories will signal that these cultures are to be avoided and not only will they lose their high-performing or high-potential employees, it will affect recruitment of new people too. In my experience, the half-life of a toxic culture is likely to be between five to 20 years depending on the meaningful action taken. And without being able to retain or recruit talent, generate stability and therefore provide consistent high performance, delivery of strategy is very hard to achieve and the reputation of the company will continue to suffer until such time as the reputation of the company's culture is restored. According to a recent report from MIT Sloan, using over 1.4m employee reviews to analyse working conditions, they found that toxic culture is 10 times more powerful than compensation in predicting turnover and that this turnover costs US businesses alone nearly $50bn a year.[26]

And it gets worse.

The problems caused by toxic cultures aren't just limited to the workplace. They have also been proved to cause people to behave poorly towards their loved ones too.[27] While many may not take physical work home with them, they will undoubtedly take the emotion of it with them.

If you've ever had an argument with a friend or family member after a 'bad day' at work, you will know exactly what I mean. Your partner will often end these conversations by saying something like 'It's pointless telling me this, you have to tell your boss', to which you'll likely scream, 'I CAN'T!' Toxic cultures don't just affect your working relationships, they affect your home life too.[28]

Why bother building culture?

At this point, you may be making an assumption that toxic culture is an inevitability; that it's going to happen at some point and it's about having a plan to deal with it. However, toxic culture is not necessarily inevitable but if you start from a position of fear, then at least you're paying attention.

Great workplaces go out of their way to deliberately build culture so as to dramatically reduce the opportunity for toxicity. Great workplaces, however, seem to be increasingly rare, with only a fifth of the global workforce saying that they experience a consistently vibrant culture.[29] And that's simply not good enough, especially when you consider that at least a third of human life is spent working. Is it too much to ask for our employers to actually put time, thought, money and effort into creating a respectful place to work? It would appear so for most.[30]

What makes the situation even more confusing is that workplace culture continues to be the key determinant of team and organization success. This isn't just a line that I thought that I'd add to justify writing this book based on an obscure piece of research conducted using a small sample size in a country far, far away. It's a fact. Almost every piece of research or review material you can find that centres on what it takes to continually achieve results will provide you with the same answer.

'When the mental health of workers suffers, so does workplace productivity, creativity, and retention' – Office of the US Surgeon General[31]

'Culture is identified ... as the largest barrier to realizing the promise of digital business' – Gartner[32]

'Culture is the number one determinant of team and organizational success' – Journal of Organizational Behaviour[33]

'Although there are processes and safeguards in place [to deal with bullying, harassment and discrimination in sport], the right culture is still required to ensure they work' – Dame Tanni Grey-Thompson, Duty of Care in Sport[34]

'According to our recent global survey of 3,200 workers in more than 40 countries, strong cultures drive better business outcomes. In fact, the majority (69 per cent) of senior leaders credit much of their success during the pandemic to culture' – PwC Global Culture Survey

In short, when companies put time, thought, money and effort into defining culture they not only reduce the risk of it becoming toxic, they also gain the following benefits:[35]

- Greater accountability
- Reduced attrition
- Increased collaboration

- Improved communication
- Increased creativity
- Increased productivity
- Better service delivery
- More trust between employees
- Better able to have courageous conversations
- Better target achievement; and
- Improved profitability.

For some more specific examples, let's turn to Fortune 100's Best Companies to Work For Survey. This annual survey provides a ranking of companies based on employee feedback and satisfaction. It evaluates factors such as employee benefits, career development opportunities, work/life balance, diversity and inclusion, and overall employee satisfaction. The responses are then analysed and the companies are ranked based on the results.

The list is highly regarded and often seen as an indicator of companies that prioritize employee well-being and maintain positive work cultures. It serves as a valuable resource for job seekers and employers alike, providing insights into companies that offer exceptional workplace experiences.

In 2023, the top 10 companies, listed at the best places to work were:[36]

1. Cisco
2. Hilton Worldwide Holdings
3. American Express
4. Wegmans Food Markets
5. Accenture
6. Nvidia
7. Atlassian
8. Salesforce
9. Comcast
10. Marriott International

On average they saw their revenue increase by almost 30 per cent year-on-year, with the mean increase being US$38bn.[37] All through building and continually evolving an environment that enables people to bring their best self to work (emotional intelligence) and where these people are committed to contributing to the team and ultimately the success of the organization (engagement).

I've worked with two of the top 10 organizations on the list and I can say from first-hand experience that they spend a lot of time thinking, planning and delivering working conditions from which these results can grow. It's no accident; they recognize that when people feel able to be their best and feel connected to something, then the results will follow.

These two factors will provide insight, at any time, into what kind of culture a team has. The four culture types can be described as follows:

Stagnant (low emotional intelligence, low engagement)

Little to nothing happens in stagnant cultures. Employees don't care about the company or the people around them. They are not interested in bettering themselves and often it feels like they only show up in order to get paid. They are not interested in goals and want conditions that suit them, rather than what's best for the team. Communication is almost non-existent and team members pay lip service to everything that comes their way.

Signs of a stagnant culture include:

- Selfish employees
- No communication between team members
- No clear strategy or vision
- No energy or drive
- No initiative
- Excessive sick leave
- No consequence for poor behaviour or performance
- Hero mentality ('Only I can do this').

Pleasant (high emotional intelligence, low engagement)

People are generally nice to each other in pleasant cultures. As emotional intelligence is high, they want to be the best version of themselves and look to build harmonious environments. Unfortunately, these environments lack a determination to hit targets or get work done. People want to believe that goals can be achieved but spend far too much time either working on lower-value work, putting barriers in the way of the work that needs to be done, or by ensuring that every single person is included in every single decision.

Signs of a pleasant culture include:

- Taking the time to build relationships
- Ensuring that there is maximum inclusion
- Understanding (but not necessarily following) the right way to do things
- Blind optimism
- Decision avoidance
- Unclear priorities
- Over-consultation
- Easy-to-achieve targets.

Combatant (low emotional intelligence, high engagement)

By contrast with pleasant cultures, people in combatant cultures act inhumanely towards each other. While performance may be high (as a result of high engagement in the work), behaviours often leave much to be desired. Workloads are high as is stress, anxiety and pressure to deliver. People have little time for each other, play 'politics', strive for power and authority, and use friction to generate actions. Expectations are unrealistic and employees are expected to be available whenever the work needs to be done.

Signs of a combatant culture include:

- Clear strategy and targets
- Commitment to the company

- Fear
- Blame
- Excessive stress or mental health leave
- Everything is deemed to be a top priority
- Aggressiveness (overt and passive)
- Swearing.

Vibrant (high emotional intelligence, high engagement)

High performance occurs consistently in vibrant cultures. In these environments, people not only feel able to bring their best self to their work, they are also surrounded by those who feel likewise. There is a complete commitment to achievement of the vision, which is clear and unambiguous in a way that supports the values of the company. Respectful relationships are built and maintained through healthy friction and diversity of thought. Success is celebrated and the team looks to continually improve the way they do things.

Signs of a vibrant culture include:

- Achievable, stretch targets
- Takes time to define how the work will get done
- Employees who work hard at what they do
- Commitment to the team
- Growth mindset/emotional resilience
- No tolerance of 'brilliant jerks' (i.e. people who are technically good, yet behaviourally poor)
- Social interaction
- Celebrates achievement.

Vibrant cultures are great places to work, where people feel a sense of belonging. They really care about their work and believe that, through commitment to the team, anything is possible.

When employees feel a sense of belonging to the team that they're part of, then they are 90 per cent more likely to recommend their company as a great place to work as opposed to 9 per cent who don't feel the same sense of care.[38] In this scenario, employees are filled with intrinsic motivation, which is the act of doing work without any clear external rewards. People do it because it's interesting, motivating or enjoyable, as opposed to being driven by any outside incentive or pressure.

In vibrant cultures, if people don't behave respectfully towards other human beings or let the team down with their performance, they are helped and coached first. However, if they don't improve, they are moved on.

Working in these environments requires high amounts of *persevilience*. This was a word coined recently by Alastair Campbell, former Director of Communications to then UK Prime Minister, Tony Blair. It mixes the words perseverance and resilience, and for me (having worked in and with many vibrant cultures), it perfectly sums up the requirements of individuals who want to succeed. Having said that, Campbell himself, while a (now) fantastic advocate for mental health awareness, is alleged to have presided over a culture of fear during his time in politics[39]. So much so that his behaviour was used as the blueprint for the character Malcolm Tucker[40] in the hit BBC comedy series, *The Thick of It*.[41]

The Thick of It is a show that popularized toxic culture for the benefit of entertainment (see also the Gordon Ramsay vehicle, *Hell's Kitchen*). *Thick of It* writer Armando Iannucci was dismayed at this, saying in an interview, 'I stopped doing *The Thick of It* because politicians were seeing it as some sort of training manual rather than a warning.' He went on to say, 'I thought they no longer saw it as something to be embarrassed about; they saw it as something to admire, so I had failed totally and should stop.'[42]

Vibrant cultures, through their commitment to continual improvement, transparency, humility and performance are the least likely to become toxic overnight. The work that they do continues to de-risk the chance for toxicity while safeguarding performance, but it doesn't remove the possibility altogether.

This is something that 11-time championship-winning basketball head coach Phil Jackson was keen to stress in his book, *11 Rings*, 'The year after winning a championship is the hardest. That's when everybody's ego rears its head and the uncanny chemistry the team felt just a few months earlier suddenly dissolves into thin air.' Having said that, awareness generally leads to action to ensure that this doesn't happen. Action will also help to keep the organization's performance where it needs to be, its reputation intact and out of the courtroom.

So how does culture turn toxic?

Toxic culture arises when the prevailing culture of a team is consistently combatant. At that point, poor behaviour has become normalized and while progress may still be made, there is consistent gossip, rumours and a general sense that things are wrong. If no action is taken to address the issues at this point, then the toxic line is likely to be crossed and where the culture lands depends on the severity of the behaviour being displayed.

When the culture becomes corrosive the toxicity bubbles to the surface and employees (and sometimes stakeholders) are openly talking about it; it may even make it into the news at this point. It is still possible to rectify a corrosive culture, but there is a very short time period in which to do so, so immediate action is key.

When the culture becomes harmful then there is almost no way back that doesn't involve widespread resignations or the removal of senior leaders. People's lives are irrevocably impacted at this level and the impact can be catastrophic on a personal, organizational or reputational level.

Level 0: Consistently Combatant
------------The Toxic Line------------
Level 1: Corrosive
Level 2: Harmful

LEVEL 0: CONSISTENTLY COMBATANT

At this stage there is still a chance to deal with any issues and prevent them becoming toxic. Good employees are making noises about leaving often as a result of the behaviour of just one person. There may be gossip between employees about these individual behaviours or dynamics, however, the team is still performing and the media have not been notified. HR are usually aware of issues at this point and may be following a process.

Characteristics that may be present:

- High stress/anxiety
- Long hours expected
- Frequent emotional outbursts
- Passive-aggressive communication
- Unconscious bias
- Microaggressions
- No acknowledgement of effort
- A lack of humility
- Rumours and hearsay
- Persistent profanities.

LEVEL 1: CORROSIVE

At this stage the culture has become toxic and is corrosive to people, reputation and results. Good employees are starting to leave, there are public outbursts, disagreements between individuals and team performance is affected. Sick leave is increasing or else people are refusing to work with the individuals at the heart of the allegations. The media are likely to be 'aware of the issues' and anonymous sources may be briefing them as they collect more evidence or else the organization is keeping quiet in the hope that it passes. HR may be taking an active role in investigating allegations.

Characteristics that may be present:

- Bullying
- Harassment
- Shouting
- Aggressive profanities
- Favouritism
- Unethical behaviour
- Persistent self-interest
- Dismissal of ideas
- Malicious gossip
- Blame and excuses.

LEVEL 2: HARMFUL

At this stage the culture is harmful to people, reputation and results. Good employees have left and have gone public about why they have done so. The culture is now a local/national media story and shareholder value or public confidence will diminish. Pressure will be brought to bear on those at the centre of the allegations or those accountable for addressing them. Depending on the severity of the accusations, law enforcement officials may be involved. An independent review may be commissioned to investigate the allegations and the culture of the company more broadly. Resignations or sacking of senior staff will be required.

Characteristics that may be present:

- Physical assault
- Emotional cruelty
- Verbal abuse
- Threats and ultimatums

- Fraud
- Lies/cover-ups
- Overt racism, sexism, transphobia, ageism
- Dismissal of concerns despite evidence
- Expectation of participation (in dangerous actions)
- Self-preservation.

As you'll read here, senior leaders have a crucial role to play in not only investing in the deliberate definition of culture, but also in continually improving it so that it never stagnates or turns toxic.

There used to be a time when leaders didn't have to think about this. In previous years, culture was a 'black box' that sat behind the brand, never to be seen in the public domain. Those days are long gone. Even investors in businesses are taking an active interest in the conditions that senior leaders create for their people. Credit Suisse is one example. In June 2022, and after some high-profile news stories, investors took the company to court, citing the fact that leaders created a toxic 'culture in which profits were prioritized over sound risk management', where executives went, 'at times, (to) unethical illegal lengths to acquire and retain high-revenue customers', which resulted 'in a series of very public scandals'.[43] It's also worth pointing out that you can take culture too far, and rather than create a toxic culture, you create a cult instead.

Of course, cults are generally really bad things. Notable cults would include the Manson family, the Branch Davidians and the People's Temple. The latter was led by Jim Jones and led to the tragic Jonestown Massacre,[44] where he convinced over 900 people to drink soda laced with cyanide. In reporting on this, the media likened the event to the people 'drinking the Kool-Aid', which has now entered our lexicon as a metaphor for workplace cultures where people will believe anything that they're told and willingly follow a charismatic leader. In these kinds of cultures, people often give up who they are for what they do and who they're doing it for.

Often these kinds of cultures drive high performance, something that author Jim Collins spoke of in his book, *From Good to Great*, saying, 'A cult-like culture can actually enhance a company's ability to pursue Big Hairy Audacious Goals, precisely because it creates that sense of being part of an elite organization that can accomplish just about anything.' However, when it generates behaviour that undermines workplace safety and leads to the alienation of others, then results will be adversely affected, particularly when this behaviour is driven from the top.

The most recent case study for this is WeWork. I recently watched the 2021 documentary *WeWork: Or the Making and Breaking of a $47 Billion Unicorn*[45] and the culture on show was cult-like in every dimension. From the free food and bizarre team rituals to the days of partying in remote places, owner Adam Neumann sought to hoodwink not only staff but also investors with his claim that WeWork was a technology (and not a real estate) company. Yet hundreds of employees and investors alike bought into it.

Neumann was talking a language that they wanted to understand. He was building a belief system that they wanted to adopt and was using his charisma to draw more and more people in. Of course, the WeWork story ended badly for Neumann. His failure to elucidate a coherent strategy (see next chapter) from which to build a sustainable, safe corporate culture led to his removal as CEO. It also ended badly for WeWork itself which – despite the commitment of Japanese financial institution SoftBank filed for bankruptcy in November 2023.[46]

So how do you spot whether you have a culture or a cult? Here are some signs:

- You use a language or terminology that no one understands
- You have a charismatic leader who can do no wrong
- Feedback is discouraged and/or ignored
- No one questions cultural norms that alienate others

- People are made to feel guilty for not 'joining in'
- Commitment is questioned when people don't adopt (often unproductive) cultural norms
- The team culture doesn't conform to the organization's values, philosophies or principles.

The actions that managers can take to avoid (consciously or unconsciously) building a cult are as follows:

- Ask yourself whether the culture is *about* you or whether it *contains* you
- Don't create acronyms or build systems that only you and your incumbent team understand
- Ensure that new members of the team are hired to challenge and improve existing ways of doing things rather than conform to them
- Avoid events and rituals that seek to make the team *look* unique
- Define your team culture to be in line with that of the organization, not adjunct to it.

In his book, *Corporate Cults, The Insidious Lure of the All-Consuming Organization*,[47] author Dave Arnott said, 'Corporate cults are like dysfunctional families in which there are no boundaries between the individual member and the family.' He's right: boundaries create safety, transparency, accountability and ultimately lead to a culture of continual improvement for all, not just for the personalities and egos that cults have been created to enhance.

There are many organizations continually selling the specialness of their culture, but if you have to give up your identity to be admitted then they are never worth joining. Drinking the Kool-Aid is not a wellness tool, it is the antithesis of it.

Detox your culture: actions

When employees want to work, want to contribute and want to help others, then they create the cultural conditions for success. By far the easiest and best way to avoid a toxic culture is to ensure staff are involved in the definition and continual evolution of culture.

When employees themselves are able to spot the kind of culture that they have, they are more likely to speak up and work with each other to address where they believe they are letting themselves down. However, managers still have the responsibility for keeping a watchful eye on the culture of the team every single hour of every single day. Being passive when it comes to culture will either lead to stagnation or toxicity and both of those will lead to good staff leaving, results being missed and increase the potential for negative publicity.

Five things:

1. Be a good human and a positive force for good within your culture.
2. Deliberately build team culture every year to meet the challenges or opportunities that you have.
3. Educate staff on the different types of cultures so that they understand what action to take to get to (and stay) vibrant.
4. If you notice any signs of toxicity, take immediate action to address it.
5. If you have any cults developing in your organization, ensure that the manager stays aligned to the values of the organization and shares what works with everyone else.

CHAPTER TWO

What's the plan?

'Ubisoft is a group that places the well-being of its teams at the heart of its strategy. The Group is strongly committed to developing a business culture that promotes the fulfilment of every individual.'

Ubisoft 2021 Registration Document[1]

It's easy to state in a 348-page document that you place well-being at the heart of your strategy in the hope of providing fulfilment to every individual. And quite another to do it in practice.

Ubisoft's 2021 Universal Registration Document sought to draw a line under the issues that it faced the year prior when allegations of abuse, as reported in an investigation by French publication *Le Télégramme*,[2] led to a wave of court cases, resignations and sackings. It's fair to say that the (predominantly male-dominated) gaming industry doesn't have a great reputation for culture and that Ubisoft is just one of many that has appeared in the media in the last few years.

Reports of the behaviour of many members of staff made the news around the world, with its Singapore office being alleged as 'one of the worst studios in terms of culture'.[3] To their credit, they undertook a review and replaced their head of HR and established a new VP to head up diversity and inclusion in the hope of building a new culture. However, to rebuild a culture requires much more than a couple of new people and a determination to put well-being at the heart of your strategy.

Rebuilding the culture needs to *become* the strategy and that's very hard for senior leaders to fathom in a world dominated by a traditional strategic focus of financial goals and the win-at-all-costs approach required to deliver them. Many leaders still expect culture to just happen without the need for any investment.

Fulfilment of every individual requires more than just sending everyone on a course to teach them what sexual harassment is and isn't (as Ubisoft did). It requires that individuals who were culpable are removed from their positions, it requires education and it requires time and money to be spent on a continual evolution program that includes every single member of the organization.

A spokesperson from Ubisoft provided an update following a report to say that little had changed: 'Additional initiatives are underway and are being rolled out over the coming months. We are committed to strengthening our culture and values in the long term, to help ensure every team member at Ubisoft is heard, respected and valued in the workplace.'[4]

Their Universal Document states, 'the Board contributes to the determination of the Group's objectives and strategy in line with its culture and values.' Hopefully, they understand what that means, but I'm not confident.[5] It's one thing to write words in a strategy document and something quite different to spend time and money over many years, righting the wrongs that have come before it.

Nissan's toxic culture developed as a result of a strategy that concentrated power at the top and stifled dissent. The company's former CEO (from June 2001 to April 2017), Carlos Ghosn, was known for his aggressive leadership style and centralized decision-making. This led to an environment where employees were afraid to voice concerns or challenge decisions. The lack of transparency and accountability in the leadership ranks contributed to a sense of mistrust and frustration among employees. Ghosn's arrest over allegations of fraud in 2018 exposed deeper issues within the company's culture and governance.[6]

Despite the challenges to that automotive industry brought about as a result of the COVID-19 pandemic, Nissan managed to improve its profits by 52 per cent year on year in 2022. Not only that, but employees now rate its culture highly and the new CEO has an 87 per cent approval rating, a clear sign that the business is flourishing under a renewed culture.[7][8]

Good strategy provides a detailed plan of action for any organization to achieve a set of short- to medium-term goals and this plan will be different for each type of business. Selling products, developing new ones, gaining market share, delivering public services, winning trophies/medals... strategies come in all shapes and sizes, but their focus is always on the short- to medium-term.

If the strategy time-period is too long (and I remember the days of 10-year strategies!), then not only will it require constant, time and energy-consuming revision but employees will continually question its validity or reality, both of which can lead to a toxic culture. What employees of all businesses are looking for is a clear view of what the overall plan is; something that they can believe in and that gets them excited about what they can be part of.

So then we come to the age-old question, 'What comes first, culture or strategy?' Well, it's strategy, because without it, you can't clearly articulate the culture required to deliver it. And how do we build a really good strategy? Well, through the culture, obviously!

The two are not mutually exclusive. However, without a strategy, it's really hard to define how work gets done as there are no clear objectives or goals to aim for. While your organization may be staffed by good humans with strong values, they still need leaders to provide a plan linked to a vision of what the organization wishes to become. That said, if you have people who don't want to fill in the forms, justify their projects, explain the reasoning behind their structures and budgets, turn up for meetings on time, engage in lively constructive debate with other humans, then you need to address the culture first.

Without employee cooperation and courageous conversations to reach agreement on how objectives and goals will be delivered within a given time period, then strategy is not worth the (electronic) paper that it's written on.

In late 2022, technology companies around the world started laying off staff. Lots of staff: over 150,000 and counting. According to the management teams of these organizations, they (somehow) hadn't predicted a slowdown in business growth once the COVID pandemic eased and people could meet in person again, and as a result had over-hired.

Microsoft CEO Satya Nadella explained the decision to staff in a blog in January 2023, 'as we saw customers accelerate their digital spend during the pandemic, we're now seeing them optimise their digital spend to do more with less.'[9]

I think it's nice here how Nadella blames his own consumers for Microsoft's poor decision-making. It's not their strategy or growth projections that were wrong, it's our fault for optimizing something or other, thus meaning that they stand to make a billion less profit than they originally thought. Or not.

Nadella goes on to say that 10,000 jobs would be lost, but that they 'will continue to invest in strategic areas for our future, meaning we are allocating both our capital and talent to areas of secular growth and long-term competitiveness for the company, while divesting in other areas'. Finally, he said, 'we will treat our people with dignity and respect, and act transparently.' This despite the fact that you need a Harvard degree to understand the previous point.

When Facebook parent company Meta announced their redundancies in March 2023,[10] staff issued a vote of no confidence in the people running the company. According to the *Washington Post*, only 26 per cent of staff surveyed said that they had confidence in their organization's leadership.[11] Fewer than half (46 per cent) felt valued by the organization.

Trust in leadership is crucial because if employees don't feel they are being listened to, don't understand the strategy, don't feel connected to the people around them or valued for the work that they do, then a toxic culture will more than likely ensue, leading to the loss of the very people required to turn it around.

Having spoken to a senior leader who recently left Facebook, they felt that the culture started to sour with the launch of the Metaverse, which was announced by founder Mark Zuckerberg in a blog in 2021.[12] Most staff – this leader said – saw it as no more than an exciting side project, something for Zuckerberg to 'play around' with as they sought to address the declining use of Facebook, alongside the continued development of Instagram, WhatsApp and other side projects. However, the organization then ploughed billions into the development of the Metaverse and got companies throughout the US excited about the prospect of doing likewise, only to seemingly abandon it in early 2023 with the sudden rise of ChatGPT, an artificial intelligence chatbot developed by OpenAI software.[13]

Unlike its launch, there was no blog to talk about the change in strategy or an 'Ask Me Anything' session with the founder or leadership team to clarify the priorities. They just seemed to quietly bury it in a shallow grave, leading to widespread internal confusion and the aforementioned plummet in confidence.

There's another issue that few have talked about since the tech job losses began. Many of these companies, when in hiring mode, made grand statements about their culture being similar to that of a 'family'. I understand the sentiment of trying to send a message that you're building a place of belonging, empathy and compassion, where great work can thrive.

Building 'family-style' cultures was in vogue in the early 2000s. Indeed, in their 2003 book, *The Character of a Corporation*, authors Gareth Jones and Rob Goffee wrote that these workplaces (which they called *Communal Cultures*) 'can make companies tremendously effective and the people who work for them feel immensely fulfilled'. They continued, 'It can indeed be the culture that most contributes to making an organization unbeatable.'

However, we have moved on significantly since then and came to realize that work is, well… work. If an organization tries to sell it as something other than that, then the chances of toxicity are greatly enhanced as people will look for a level of empathy, compassion and understanding that just won't be there when targets need to be hit or service levels maintained. Also, when the 'culture as family' terminology is used, the assumption is that every family is highly functional, communicates regularly with honesty and clarity, understands the line between work and home life, and treats each member with respect. How does that assumption play out for your *real* family? Maybe Douglas Coupland had it right with his 2001 book title, *All Families are Psychotic*?

Not only does the word family mean different things to different people in different cultures, but worse, when you have to let someone go – as a result of a financial or performance decision – then an employee can point the finger at you – personally, or virtually – and ask, 'is this how you treat your family?' And they'd probably be right.

This happened at many technology companies during their jobs purge in 2022/3, who'd hitherto had a good track record at investing in culture and developing strategy.

Bad strategy

Many companies, however, still struggle with the strategy development and associated approval process and this can itself be the source of toxic culture. Some examples include:

1. Unachievable goals
    Strategies are created to deliver to a set of goals and when these goals are seen as unachievable from the outset, then managers and employees will immediately disengage from the process of strategy creation. They will question the wisdom of the owners, executives or officials responsible for setting them. When these questions make it to the media, then the organization is presented in a negative light and the existing culture – as well as their reputation – is affected.

2. Overly complex process

   Sometimes the toxicity can arise as a result of the process of creating it. Many forms to be completed, submitted and approved over an incredibly long period of time. Sometimes there are just too many layers to this approval process. Just when managers feel they have completed the actions of defining their plans, project definitions and the budgets and structures to deliver these, they will be asked to revise them for less money or else define other structures to do so. Too much complexity will ultimately lead to managers disconnecting from the process and undermining the quality of the strategy as a result.

3. Unnecessary demands on people's time

   Strategy workshops, meetings, presentations and the associated documents to read and write can take up hours of management and employee time. Not to mention the follow-on meetings, revised presentations, pre-meetings before the actual meetings and endless iterations of the documents used to support them! And all of these things need to be done without compromising existing business as usual or project activity. Invariably, this will mean managers working late or at the weekend in order to keep up, which in turn will affect their emotional and physical health and generate toxicity towards those people overseeing the activities.

4. Poor communication

   The biggest issue that I saw when I was a senior manager was the utterly shocking communication around the strategy production process. At times there wasn't any communication at all, just a meeting invitation with no further information. Other times, the CEO would talk about 'progress made on the strategy production process' when we had no idea that it had been started! But often it's the meetings themselves that grind the most. Endless invitations with no context, no preparation notes, just a requirement to produce a PowerPoint of indeterminate length that may, or may not, be appropriate for the production and approval of the strategy. As a senior manager myself, I understood the need for strategy, but *how* it was communicated got to me every time.

5. Slow decision-making

Senior managers have three jobs – I'm dumbing it down, but stick with me – as follows: 1) Be a role model for great behaviour. Demonstrate the behaviours that you expect of others and be a good human by showing empathy, vulnerability, humility and discipline; 2) Understand subject matter. In order to set expectations clearly and ensure that targets are hit, it's important to be able to ask the right questions at the right time; and 3) Make decisions. Say yes or no to things based on the information presented to them so as not to impede progress.

And of course all of these things are important, but in the production and approval of strategy, decision-making is key in ensuring that the production process takes weeks, not months and that the ideas put forward are the ones that, at that moment in time, give the organization or team the best opportunity of hitting its goals. Pontification will lead to frustration and this will manifest itself in the conversations and relationships between employees, some of which will turn toxic and in extreme circumstances never be healed.

Strategy is critical to every business. It doesn't matter whether you have a five-person gardening business in Sheffield, UK, or head up a multinational technology organization in Mumbai, India, you need a set of objectives and goals to aim for and that act as a foundation to build a culture set up to deliver them. However, if the strategy is unclear, then the culture will evolve (usually negatively) to meet what is perceived to be the objectives of the organization.

A great example of this was Wells Fargo Bank in the US. In 2016, they hit the news after the Consumer Financial Protection Bureau fined them USD$185m after they were found to have fraudulently created millions of accounts without their customers' consent.[14] Customers only noticed the accounts after incurring charges for which they had no knowledge. Initial reports laid the blame squarely on branch workers, but it later transpired that senior leadership were culpable for instigating a strategy of vigorous cross-selling.[15]

The strategy was apparently the brainchild of former Wells Fargo CEO Richard M. Kovacevich, who used it extensively at his prior employer, Norwest Corporation. Kovacevich gave the impression that he was a culture-first leader in the early 1990s and regularly championed the *Wells Fargo Vision and Values*. It was published in a brochure[16] and featured comments such as:

'A good strategy perfectly executed will beat a great strategy poorly executed every time.'

'We define "culture" as knowing what you need to do when you get up in the morning without having to be told what to do.'

All pretty good stuff, particularly back then. Also included, however, was this statement:

'The core of our vision and our strategy is "cross-selling". The more we give our customers what they need, the more we know about them. The more we know about their other financial needs, the easier it is for them to bring us more of their business. The more business they do with us, the better value they receive, the more loyal they are.'

Because (also included in the brochure):

'The key to the bottom line is the top line. If we had to select only one goal, it would be revenue growth.'

This was the strategy and cross-selling that was a 'growth at all costs' approach, which became the culture of the organization. During the investigation, employees described the intense pressure that they came under to sell – often up to 20 – products, with every customer interaction.

Employees were instructed to sign existing customers up to as many products as possible to increase the revenue that the bank was able to generate (from as little as US$41 per month to thousands of dollars per month, with mortgages being the biggest earner).[17] Their sales record as a result was phenomenal and the envy of competitors across the US for years… until, however, the fraud and the stresses brought to bear upon employees were exposed. The stress led to a culture where employees were crying, experiencing severe panic attacks[18] and vomiting in the office became commonplace.[19] One person even ingested hand sanitizer to try and cope with the pressure.[20]

Employees' attempts to report the culture up the chain were ignored and many staff quit or were fired for protesting at the fraudulent practices.[21] Wells Fargo subsequently rehired about 1,000 staff – once the investigation had been completed – as these are the very people required to build a safe, honest, respectful workplace culture.

The strategy led not only to record fines and tarnished reputations but the culture continues to struggle to recover to this day. A report in 2019, three years after the scandal had been exposed, found that not much had changed at all. Comments included, '[Frontline workers] have no confidence or faith the company will improve things [until] they have an independent organization where they can safely raise concerns without retaliation' and 'Things put in place don't seem to be doing much of anything and we still hear complaints from customers.'[22]

One could argue that the bank, during this period, had a clear strategy of sell, sell, sell and sell some more. However, it was an egregious strategy that placed undue pressure on employees to commit fraud and the toxicity this created has yet to dissipate.

But where to start with building the *right* strategy on which to build a vibrant culture?

Getting strategy started

To begin with, you need the right people in the room at the right time, but not all of the people all of the time. When people don't understand why they've been invited to a workshop or else aren't asked to contribute, it will negatively affect how they feel. So it's crucial that leaders spend time thinking about the structure of the work required to build the strategy as well as the preparation needed to ensure that those workshops are a success. A friend of mine facilitates strategy development sessions and is continually staggered by the amount of time wasted as a result of poorly prepared attendees.

In his paper, *Good Strategy/Bad Strategy: The Difference and Why It Matters*, author Richard P. Rumelt reinforces this by saying, 'Good strategy is hard work and many executives either avoid it or don't really know what it entails.'

You can't cheat or shortcut the process of building a good strategy, nor can you simply list lots of goals without analysing if they can be achieved. The process to build strategy should be as simple as possible – to retain maximum engagement from those involved – and should answer these four basic questions:

1. Where are you now? This provides a context for the way forward.
2. What is your aspiration? This articulates where you want to be and by when.
3. How will you achieve this? This provides a plan of action.
4. How will you measure it? This provides the foundations for achievement.

Each of these questions needs to be addressed with clear statements, arguments, priorities and a determination on generating value and improving how you do what you do, rather than being all about 'growth'. This value will be different, based on the work that you do. However, it will provide employees with a sense of purpose and something to aim for. This will give rise to intrinsic motivation – that is, the desire to do something without the need for reward or recognition – which is the antidote to toxic culture.

When intrinsic motivation dies, it takes the culture, strategy and results with it.

Some pitfalls that get in the way of producing a coherent strategy and provide fuel for a toxic culture include:

- No connection to the vision – a disconnect between the plan and the aspiration.
- Unclear priorities – confusion surrounding what's important and what's not.
- Over-reliance on theory – thought leadership is good, slavish devotion to the latest management system (e.g. agile, SixSigma etc.) is not.
- Confusing terminology – or as Rumelt calls it, 'fluff'. Things that fail to hold up when scrutinized.
- Poor risk identification – an inability to acknowledge what could go wrong.
- Playing it safe – avoidance of the positive risks to be taken to achieve goals.
- Too much detail – over-prescription or else too many sub-strategies that lead to confusion.
- Not enough money – to do the thing that the strategy promises to do.
- Pie-in-the-sky ideas – ideas that aren't grounded in reality or else a million miles away from what you do now.
- Wanting to do more with less – this is simply not possible.
- Inflated goals – targets that are simply not achievable.
- Set and forget – the reluctance to revisit and revise strategy based on the changing nature of the business/world.
- No link to culture – *how* it will be delivered needs to be explicit in the strategy itself.

So, with all of that in mind, what does good strategy look like, such that it provides the basis for a strong culture? Here are five suggestions to help you avoid strategic toxicity:

1. Achievable goals

    In his book, *Fit for Disruption*,[23] author Matthew Webber says, 'The longer the time span [of strategy], the greater the gap between expectation and reality.' I couldn't have written this better. To be achievable, and therefore believable, the strategy has to be focused on the shorter-term goals, with a commitment to continual iteration to reach longer-term goals.

    As I mentioned earlier, I'm old enough to remember 10-year strategies. These were produced in a time when we didn't understand how technology would increase exponentially every year. It was a stake in the ground, with the focus on years one to three. The objectives we set dealt with the financial or customer service targets we had, but, importantly, were an improvement on the year before.

    At our best as a leadership team, we asked ourselves the following questions:

    - Was our performance last year a result of any extraordinary circumstances (positive or negative)?
    - What did we do that we hadn't done before that produced unexpected results?
    - What did we learn from the targets that we missed?
    - What conditions did we create that helped people deliver to the expectations that we set?
    - What did we decide to do away with or reject that helped our people to feel appropriately challenged to achieve our goals?
    - What unintentional roadblocks did we create as a leadership team that got in the way of target delivery?
    - Were our vision and goals clear and did they act as a motivator for employees?
    - How can we stretch our targets without burning out our people?

2. Simple to understand, define and evolve

This may come as a surprise to many people, but not everyone understands what strategy is and how it's used so prior to undertaking any kind of strategy planning work, people should be educated on strategy. Get everyone to the same level of knowledge and help them to understand their role in making it the best that it can be. Oh, and unless you want a combatant culture, stay away from the war analogies. No quotes from Sun Tzu, stories of Hannibal or use of language that talks about struggles or battles. The processes that are then used to pull the strategy together should be simple to understand so that people can deliver to the expectations that have been set.

Strategy evolves over time, so any attempt to create the *perfect* strategy should be abandoned early on in favour of creating an approach that generates immediate value and positions you advantageously for future revisions.

3. Appropriate use of people's time

And in line with the previous point, dispense yourself with complicated forms and/or PowerPoint presentations. Yes, workshops will be required to gather information, ideas, estimates and to generate excitement around what's possible, but make them engaging and run them properly.

Don't be boring and make people appreciate the time that they're giving up to work on this crucial element of business success. It should be a pleasure to work on strategy, not the pain that it generally seems to create.

Take an iterative approach. Meet little and often, focus on being better at everything you do, make decisions quickly and recognize that your strategy – in line with the world – will be dynamic.

Don't make strategy a game that people find hard to understand and utilize expertise from everywhere, not just a special few senior managers.

4. Great communication

    Every time strategy work is undertaken it creates uncertainty and generates fear. I mentioned this to a CEO earlier in 2023 and his immediate response was, 'Well, it shouldn't do.' Which – as I pointed out to him – was easy for him to say as he was involved in the activity to build it, but 95 per cent of his organization isn't.

    When people's managers suddenly disappear into long workshops and can't really talk about what they're doing, it's only natural that it will generate discussion from those not involved. The simple way to address this is through regular communication, but don't make it sound more important than it is. Don't single out the special people involved (as this may alienate those that aren't) and don't use language such as 'tough decisions', 'tighten our belts', or 'operating model reviews' until such time as the strategy has been completed and you're able to talk about them properly.

5. Efficient decision-making

    Great strategy requires efficient decision-making and that means you simply won't be able to do everything that you want to do or else you need to be ruthless about what's the most important thing right now.

    Don't create endless lists of items that have been 'carried' for decision, just get the right people in the room, have a robust discussion (if required), make a decision and move on.

    Don't get sucked into the trap of agreeing to disagree – as you still haven't resolved the issue – acknowledge people's viewpoints, make a call on which way you're going to go and ensure that everyone is behind the decision.

    Building strategy isn't a popularity contest where everyone gets an equal share. It's about delivering value for the organization, not to the whims of a CEO, government minister or an individual senior manager.

Don't forget the culture

It's also crucially important to remember that culture is a strategy in itself. If you're a CEO, then your HR or People and Culture leader has been saying this for years and – shock/horror – they're right! Who knew?

A culture strategy isn't a checklist of training courses that need to be mandated across the organization. The culture strategy talks to the work and commitment required to build a sustainable vibrant workplace that can deliver the results outlined in the strategy. And organizations are fantastic at defining goals, but not at agreeing (and then sticking to) *how* those goals will be achieved. This is where your culture strategy is critical.

HR has the responsibility for working with leaders to talk about the initiatives required to create these conditions and for pulling together a budget to allow them to do so.

While there is no universally recommended percentage for how much a company should spend on fostering a great workplace culture, in my experience of working with some of the best, investing around 1–2 per cent of the company's revenue is a good starting point. This isn't just culture definition work, it also includes the time costs for the small micro-experiences that bring culture to life every single day. Birthdays, milestone celebrations, social interactions, travel to fly people to be together and maintain connection as well as training, development, coaching and mentoring. All of these things are critical components of building and evolving a vibrant culture, but remember that if senior managers don't role model the behaviours they expect of others, it'll all be for nought! And if you're *still* not convinced, Gallup found that organizations with engaged employees outperform those with disengaged employees by 147 per cent.[24]

The signs are that many leadership teams are finally starting to see this value. Feedback from a recent survey from PwC found that, 'Of the C-suite and board members who participated in our survey,

66 per cent are even saying now that culture is more important to performance than the organization's strategy or operating model.'[25]

Southwest Airlines is a great example of an organization that has both a strong strategy and a strong culture. They were in the news at the end of 2022 as a result of extreme weather and operational issues that led to flights being grounded and customers inconvenienced and yet, at no stage did the culture become toxic. Firstly, they had a very clear strategy that they stuck to and secondly, because they spend time and money creating an environment that employees want to be part of, there was clarity in communication at all times. It was because of its culture that Southwest Airlines was able to address the issues it faced, refunded customers for their inconvenience and returned to normal operations quickly without too much reputational damage.[26]

Continually moving feast

I once had a boss who loved the term 'moving feast'. Everything for him was meals on wheels, not least strategy. I can still remember him saying to me, 'Yes, the strategy has been approved, but that just means it's already out of date. Grab your cutlery because strategy is a continually moving feast.'

The point he was making – and it was a great lesson early in my management career – is that the environment within which all business operates changes on a daily basis. Some things become more important, others become less important. Some projects get started, others finish. Money is there until it's not, similarly with customers. Strategy definition is not a 'set and forget' exercise. It requires regular check-ins to ensure continual relevance, that priorities are clear, opportunities understood and risks are being managed.

The Quarterly Business Review (QBR) is an excellent mechanism to do this. It serves as a strategic management tool to ensure that the company's goals and objectives are being met and to identify areas for improvement and growth.

The concept of regular business reviews dates back decades, but the formalization of the Quarterly Business Review gained popularity in the late twentieth century with the rise of performance management and the need for more structured and systematic assessments of a company's performance.

As businesses became more complex and competitive, the need for regular reviews to track progress and make informed decisions became evident. Today, QBRs are an integral part of corporate governance and strategic planning for organizations that understand the importance of strategic delivery to culture. The format can vary from company to company, however at the very least it should cover the following:

- Operational highlights – including any challenges faced in the previous quarter.
- Financial performance – an analysis of financial metrics such as revenue, profit margins, expenses and cash flow. This section assesses the financial health of the company and its alignment with the targets set in the strategy. Financial goals for the next three months should be agreed.
- Competitive landscape – an analysis of how the company compares to its competitors in terms of market share, product offerings and customer perception.
- Risks – an analysis of the risks that the company faces and the actions being taken (not just written down!) to mitigate them.
- Culture – a pulse check on the current culture and whether it is sufficiently vibrant to achieve the goals. This should take the form of a 'pulse check' and the key themes analysed and actioned. The culture evolution plan for the next three months should be agreed.

When Toys 'R' Us (TRU) went bankrupt in 2018, almost 30,000 employees lost their jobs. And what killed TRU was a failure of strategy. Due to a leveraged buyout in 2005 the organization saddled itself with debt that would slowly strangle its operations.[27]

The interest payments on the debt significantly constrained the company's financial flexibility and ability to invest in necessary improvements to its stores and online platforms as online shopping became increasingly popular. As e-commerce grew in popularity and consumers became more tech-savvy, TRU fell further behind and in the court filing for bankruptcy, they blamed organizations such as Walmart, Target and (of course) Amazon, stating that they 'could not compete'.[28]

Yet, had their senior leadership team and board of directors met regularly to focus on the evolving needs of the marketplace and devised sensible strategies for servicing their debt, building experiences that matched customer expectations, all while laying the groundwork for a twenty-first-century business, they might never have gone into liquidation. And of course, because money was tight, they made the ultimate mistake: they cut staffing costs. Key staff left, offices became dirty as cleaning contracts were cancelled and employees started to lie on staff surveys to give the impression of high store performance.[29]

TRU is now used as a case study – alongside Nokia and Kodak – of an organization whose management developed an 'it won't happen to us' mentality and paid the ultimate price.

Detox your culture: actions

Strategy is crucial not only to articulating the company's objectives and goals, but also in providing the context and plan for the culture required to do so. The activity required to build and evolve it should be approached professionally, but in a way that generates engagement. I can usually get a sense of an organization's culture through the way that people talk about the strategy or how it is presented to me ahead of any work that I may be doing.

Keep it simple, achievable and have a plan to continually evolve it. Quarterly strategy reviews work well. Not only to assess whether you're on track to deliver the value as planned, but also whether you need to work on the culture to ensure that you do so.

Toxic culture is the biggest risk to strategy delivery because when employees become disengaged from the work that they're doing, productivity will slow, sickness and attrition will increase and all the money in the world won't be able to fix the reputational problem that you have.

Success starts with strategy, but it gets delivered through culture.

Five things:

1. Take the time – but not too much time! – working with teams to build strategy to deliver the vision that the organization has defined.
2. Continually review it – quarterly works well – to ensure that priorities are understood and it remains fit for purpose.
3. Keep the process simple and bureaucracy-free.
4. Communicate the strategy in a way that builds excitement about *how* it will be delivered.
5. Ensure that you include your culture strategy – which also requires funding and a plan to positively evolve it through the strategy period.

CHAPTER THREE

What good are you doing?

'Last week was terrible. We started with policy changes that
felt simple, reasonable, and principled, and it blew things up
culturally in ways we never anticipated.'

Jason Fried, co-founder, 37 Signals

Purpose in its simplest form is the good that individuals or organizations want to do in their field/country/the world. It is also an album by Justin Bieber. For clarification, this chapter is about the former, but feel free to listen to the latter while reading it.

Like most things in the world of work today, it wasn't really a thing for those of us who started work pre-2000s. When I took my first job in 1987, I was working as a teller for a bank and it was reinforced to me regularly that the bank's job – and therefore mine – was to make new money and safeguard the money we already had, which I suppose is a purpose of sorts.

It's just that a purpose wasn't written down in a pithy sentence and plastered all over the walls, annual report or wheeled out in media statements when senior people behaved unethically. And it wasn't something that I personally gave any thought to either – I just wanted money to buy records and beer. Hey, I was 17, what did you expect?!

Except 17-year-olds entering the workforce today have a different set of morals, ideals and expectations and are growing up in a world that's much changed to the one that I experienced – a fact that continues to be lost on many employees my age. There are threats to the environment, many are saddled by debts incurred as a result of their education, most can't afford to get onto the property ladder and (at the time of writing), wages aren't growing in line with the cost of living. So, it's only right that, at a minimum, they'd be looking for something different from their employers and research shows that Millennial and Gen Z workers value purpose almost as much as they do pay; for many, it's a key determinant as to whether they join an organization or not.[1]

It's not enough anymore for an organization to offer a good salary and benefits with the option of some flexibility. They must also stand for something and actively demonstrate this on a daily basis.

Purpose is not a generational fad, it is the realization that, according to scholars, purpose is 'central to one's satisfaction in their work lives and career'.[2] I haven't spoken to a human being yet who doesn't want to feel valued, be a good team member, hit their targets or deadlines AND do good in the world. Research shows that this is also the pathway to greater happiness and well-being.[3] Some parents of these young adults realize this and are actively encouraging them to 'find their purpose' or 'do something that lights them up'. Which is very different from the advice given to most Gen-X children.

When humans feel connected to their work it leads to greater engagement, greater collaboration, higher job satisfaction and increased loyalty. All critically important attributes for organizations that are looking to do more with less in a talent-poor market.[4] And talent retention is a huge challenge for organizations, with only about 15 per cent attracting and retaining quality candidates well.[5]

These candidates are looking for something more than process-oriented, shallow task-oriented transactions. They're looking for opportunities for growth so that they can fulfil their potential, while contributing to something that's bigger than themselves. Again, it's very easy to be cynical about these kinds of statements, yet this kind of ambition is critical to ensure that cultures don't become toxic and that businesses continue to thrive in the medium to long term.

Indeed, organizations that don't live their stated purpose are being called out around the world by their own employees. Not just on websites such as Glassdoor, but also in organized – and very public – demonstrations. According to a survey by law firm Herbert Smith Freehills,[6] employee activism, as it's called, could cost organizations up to 25 per cent of their global revenue each year due to the disruptive nature of strikes and reputational damage leading to lost business.

Organizations that have faced activism from employees for not living up to their purpose include Google,[7] Amazon[8] and 37 Signals (who make the tool Basecamp)[9] to name but a few of the high-profile examples that have made it into the news.

The 37 Signals/Basecamp story is an interesting case study. For years, founders Jason Fried and David Hansson prided themselves on creating vibrant workplace culture and even published bestselling books – much lauded by myself! – talking about the work that they did. And yet, almost overnight, they lost a third of their workforce (20 out of 57 employees according to a report in the *New York Times*[10]) and hit the news because employees felt (that by banning freedom of expression, particularly around political views), they had seemingly compromised on what they stood for. That's how quickly things can change.

Saying you stand for one thing and acting another way is one of the fastest ways to erode trust with employees. Let's face it, it also looks really bad to customers, stakeholders and the very people that organizations are looking to attract to maintain their vibrant cultures.

In a blog Fried apologized to Basecamp employees for the organization's misstep saying, 'Last week [w/c 26th April 2021] was terrible. We started with policy changes that felt simple, reasonable, and principled, and it blew things up culturally in ways we never anticipated.' He continued, 'David and I completely own the consequences, and we're sorry. We have a lot to learn and reflect on, and we will.'[11] And while that doesn't change what happened or remove the stories from the news, the two men showed humility and a willingness to improve moving forward.

Employees as activists

Not every organization takes employee activism seriously and yet they will need to. More than ever, employees are continually looking at how the company that they work for is delivering on its promise not only to them, but also to the world at large. And if they don't like what they see, they will mobilize.

Ben & Jerry's is a great example of a business that takes employee activism seriously. The ice-cream maker has a head of global activism[12] with responsibility for advancing social justice through the day-to-day operations of the business. Any organization can choose to do the same thing. Instead of fearing employee activism, there is a real opportunity to empower employees and demonstrate to stakeholders and customers that they truly stand for something, with actions behind the words. Keeping employee activism outside of the culture creates division and can even end up pitting teams and functions against each other, which ultimately leads to new layers of toxicity.

The greatest agents for change already exist within organizations. Senior managers should look for ways to bring people together, from all levels of the business; from out in the field to the shop floor, the post room to the boardroom. By creating an Employee Activism Coalition from different levels, units and regions, they can gain access to a varied set of perspectives and influence channels, as well as garnering broad support for purpose-led initiatives.

Purpose for any organization, therefore, is incredibly important and not something that can be shortcut, handed to consultants or constructed by cutting pictures out of magazines at an overtly expensive senior management retreat. When purpose is embedded into day-to-day operations, then a company is four times more likely to hit and/or exceed its financial targets and almost five times more likely to keep its existing customers and attract new ones.[13]

Consulting organization PwC have noted its importance and established a chief purpose and inclusion officer role[14] to ensure that they strive to connect an individual's values and behaviours to the purpose that PwC seek to achieve. Virgin is another example of an organization that is taking purpose seriously. Former Purpose and People Experience Director Charlotte Goodman said, 'Our purpose should drive our decisions and fuel our success.'[15]

What's your bottom line?

Success, for many leadership teams, is still measured as the 'bottom line'. Both PwC and Virgin are just two examples of companies that recognize the emerging criticality of purpose as a consideration of a successful business and the changing nature of the bottom line.

In 1994, author John Elkington coined the phrase 'triple bottom line' (TBL). Elkington described the TBL of People, Planet and Profit, saying that it 'focuses corporations not just on the economic value that they add, but also on the environmental and social value that they add – or destroy'. Essentially, it was a way of measuring how a business performs in areas other than financial returns.[16]

Most recently, this work gave rise to the Environmental, Social and Governance (ESG) framework that we see being undertaken by organizations around the world today. ESG centres around 'accountability and the implementation of systems and processes to manage a company's impact, such as its carbon footprint and how it treats employees, suppliers and other stakeholders'.[17]

In 2014, author and social commentator Ayman Sawaf, in his book, *Sacred Commerce: A Blueprint for a New Humanity*, introduced a fourth element to the TBL, that of Purpose. His assertion was that as well as delivering on financial, social and environmental promises, it should also contribute to the happiness and development of people (both employees and stakeholders alike). This became known as the Fourth Bottom Line or Quadruple Bottom Line.

The goal of adding purpose to the TBL is to encourage organizations to enhance their transparency and responsibility in developing people and equipping them with the necessary capabilities and attitudes for the future. For clarity, the four Ps are as follows:

- Purpose: The good that the organization seeks to do in the world.
- People: The value and quality of life the organization creates for its employees, customers and community.
- Planet: The positive impact the organization is making to the environment.
- Profit: The financial performance of the organization.

Organizations that do this in an authentic way, can expect to achieve the following benefits over and above the traditional TBL measures:

- Increased engagement and productivity
- Retain high-potential employees
- Become an employer of choice
- Boost stakeholder support and engagement
- Continual sustainable growth.

When purposeful engagement with employees and stakeholders is embraced it is seen as market leading, not only in results but also through the way in which those results are achieved.

Outdoor apparel business Patagonia is a great example of an organization that has embraced the four Ps. Started by American rock climber and environmentalist Yvon Chouinard in 1973, the organization was cited in audits – and an article in the *Atlantic* in 2015[18] – for labour abuses and set about changing the ways in which they work.

From addressing those labour concerns to a nine-fold increase in its commitments to corporate social responsibility to providing childcare for its workers, the leadership team at Patagonia have set about not only creating a strong, self-sufficient business, but also one that is focused on its contribution to the environment and to building a great place to work.

It commits 1 per cent of its sales to groups that campaign for the environment and even led a boycott of the Outdoor Retailer show in Utah in 2017 because of the state's stance on the transfer of federal lands to the state. The cause garnered considerable support, leading to the show being moved to Colorado.[19]

At the time of writing this book, Patagonia has a Glassdoor score of 4.3 (out of 5), with an earlier survey finding that 91 per cent of employees say that it's a great place to work.[20]

Purpose vs vision

The biggest challenge I continue to find is confusion around what a purpose is and how it should be used. And if senior managers don't understand it, then no one else will either. Indeed, while 82 per cent of respondents in one survey attested to the importance of purpose, less than half (42 per cent) said that their purpose had much effect day-to-day.[21]

If the purpose is confusing to employees, then not only will performance be continually affected, but decision-making will be flawed and undermine almost every area of the business. For a purpose to mean anything, people need to understand how it is enacted in the micro-moments between employees on a day-to-day basis. So let's clear that confusion up to remove at least one of the factors that may contribute to a toxic culture and also to provide some clarity on how it differs/aligns to an organization's vision.

A purpose statement is a short statement that links the good that the organization seeks with the work that they do. For example, Campbell's Soups' purpose is Connecting people through food they love. A purpose is made public and used as a way to attract those who share a similar desire. So, if food is your passion and you enjoy working for a company that seeks to use its position and influence in the market to connect people, then Campbell's Soups might be the place for you.

However, a purpose is different to a vision. A vision is an aspirational, yet achievable statement of the future. It is generally used as the foundation for the strategy of the organization and is a short, memorable statement used as a basis for decision-making on day-to-day activity. A good example of a vision statement might be that of Netflix: 'We aspire to entertain the world.' Do they entertain the world right now? Is it possible for them to do so? Well, yes. But different decisions will need to be made (e.g. opening up an ad-sponsored version of the platform, which they've recently done) in order to do so.

A vision should be reset every three to five years in line with the strategy, but the purpose is only ever really refreshed when there's a major change to operations, i.e. when an organization chooses to do something different. So, unlike the vision, the purpose rarely changes. But in order to provide staff, customers and stakeholders with clarity on what your business is trying to achieve then you need both. You can't just have one and hope for the best, or combine them both in the hope that people get what you're about.

The Coca-Cola Company is a good example of this – they have both a purpose and a vision:

- **Purpose:** Refresh the world, make a difference.
- **Vision:** To craft the brands and choice of drinks that people love, to refresh them in body and spirit. And done in ways that create a more sustainable business and better shared future that makes a difference in people's lives, communities and our planet.

The purpose is actually OK, although it does read a bit like a marketing statement; the vision, however, is a complete mess. Too long to ever be memorable and actually a mix of a vision and a purpose. You could (and should) end it after the first sentence because after that, it turns into a long-winded purpose statement. They could simplify both as follows:

- **Purpose:** Refreshing and making a difference to the world.
- **Vision:** To deliver drinks that people love, sustainably.

When you provide this level of clarity to managers and employees they understand not only what the organization needs to be remembered for (purpose), but also a mechanism to identify the work that it needs to do now to get it further along the path to being able to do so (vision).

British pharmaceutical and biotechnology company GlaxoSmithKline Beecham are an example that have the mix just about right:

- **Purpose:** Help people to do more, live longer, feel better.
- **Vision:** We unite science, technology and talent to get ahead of disease together.

Here are some other examples of good purpose statements (correct at the time of writing):

Ford Motor Company – To help build a better world, where every person is free to move and pursue their dreams.

Foot Locker – To inspire and empower youth culture.

Southwest Airlines – Connect People to what's important in their lives through friendly, reliable and low-cost air travel.

Target – To help all families discover the joy of everyday life.

Walgreens Boots Alliance – More joyful lives through better health.

ING – Empowering people to stay a step ahead in life and in business.

And here are a couple of very average examples of a purpose (correct at the time of writing):

GE – We rise to the challenge of building a world that works. (Too generic)

MasterCard – Connecting Everyone to Priceless Possibilities. (More of a marketing statement than a purpose)

Here are some good examples of vision statements (again, correct at the time of writing):

IKEA – To create a better everyday life for the many people.

Foot Locker – To create unrivalled experiences for our customers.

Kellogg's – A good and just world, where people are not just fed but fulfilled.

Southwest Airlines – To be the world's most loved, most efficient and most profitable airline.

New Zealand All Blacks – Inspiring and unifying through rugby.

You can't fake purpose

Having a coherent purpose statement is no guarantee that it's actually being adhered to or demonstrated on a daily basis, however. Organizations that do 'check-box culture' – where they spend time on producing purpose, vision, mission statements etc., without understanding why they are important – are usually the worst culprits. They don't understand or anticipate the negative media reaction when they have a purpose that they actively choose to ignore.

Failed pharmaceutical company Theranos are a good example of this. Their purpose was to 'make actionable information accessible to everyone at the time it matters'.[22] Despite owner Elizabeth Holmes not fully understanding how to achieve this, the venture capital world and the U.S. Food and Drug Administration bought into it anyway. Hey, if it's written down, it's definitely going to happen, right? Er, no.

In 2022, Holmes was found guilty of fraud and sentenced to 11 years in prison.[23]

Boeing's purpose is 'To protect, connect and explore our world and beyond', yet in 2018 and 2019, the 737-Max airliner was grounded around the world after two crashes killed almost 350 people in Indonesia and Ethiopia. When the investigation was completed in 2019, it found a litany of errors, not only with the airlines operating the planes but also with Boeing production and quality processes. The report found that Boeing was able to design and test its own system without proper oversight or a thorough safety assessment from the Federal Aviation Administration (FAA).[24]

Which is certainly not what you'd expect from an organization that seeks to protect.

In October 2019, then Boeing CEO Dennis Muilenburg testified in front of a senate committee and claimed not to know about the safety issues of the aircraft, despite witnesses claiming otherwise. His apologies brought further anger and scrutiny to the organization and its safety culture and he was eventually fired, two months later.[25]

Boeing paid out US$20bn in fines, fees and compensation and lost an estimated $60bn in cancelled orders. Doubts still linger about the safety culture at Boeing – further compounded (as this book was being finalized) by a door that fell off an Alaskan Airlines 737-Max mid-air – and in the high-stakes world of airline safety, this will always be bad for business.[26] [27]

It's tricky. Humans make mistakes – that's the nature of who we are and, of course, that's how we learn. Not every mistake leads to catastrophe or the loss of human life, but from time to time it does and that's a tragedy, particularly for those who lose loved ones. However, the point here is that if a company is going to state that it stands for something, then it has to follow through on that promise in everything that it does. It can't just assume that by getting a senior leader to write about how great the purpose is,[28] all employees are going to think, 'Great, I know exactly what this means to me and my job and I'll ensure that I live this purpose every day.' It's not about 'rolling' the purpose out or by putting it on screen savers, mouse mats or office walls; it's about educating staff or better still, involving them in the process of defining the purpose so that they're able to educate their teams too.

As with all culture activity, to ensure that the risk of toxicity is mitigated, purpose (and vision) definition is best done with a group of people that represents the workforce: people across all departments and who encompass all types of roles. For start-ups, this tends to be a lot easier (but no less important) as there are fewer people. For larger, global companies, greater thought needs to be given as to who this group is and also how the message around application of the purpose is disseminated. For many organizations this is both a great challenge and a huge opportunity, and different approaches can be taken.

For one global organization that I worked with, we brought 200 representatives (of all roles and levels) from around the world to take part in two days of culture building activity in the US. An incredible initiative and at least a dozen people that I spoke to afterwards said that it is something that they'll never forget.

For another, we ran a series of national events and then had a much smaller group of 'Culture Catalysts' (again of all levels) come together to use the information provided to determine the final purpose statement. In this scenario, every employee in the organization had an opportunity to contribute.

However you decide to do it, remember that to do it well, it should *feel* like hard work. If it's easy – and here, I'll return to the nonsense of senior managers cutting pictures out of magazines – then you have to question whether it's really going to give you the outcomes that you're looking for, or if you're just lazily ticking the purpose box on your culture checklist.

Detox your culture: actions

Being purpose-led not only means taking on multiple viewpoints and engaging in a structured activity to produce something meaningful, but also ensuring that every single employee knows what it means to *live* the purpose within their role. Once that is achieved, then the organization can be considered to be leading with purpose. Anything else and it's likely that they have laid some pretty strong toxic foundations, which will eventually affect engagement, productivity, reputation and ultimately, results.

The vision is a constant North Star that should ignite excitement for the future that the organization is working towards. People should be able to draw a straight line between the work that they do and how it contributes to the success of the organization. When they have this, engagement will always be high, which is a key requirement for vibrant culture.

Five things:

1. Be clear about what you stand for as an organization.
2. Don't turn purpose into a branding or marketing exercise, it needs to be something that others can measure you on.
3. Involve staff in the creation of the vision for maximum engagement.
4. Ensure that the vision is short and easy to remember.
5. Regularly check on the actions the organization is taking to live its purpose.

CHAPTER FOUR

Are you set up to succeed?

'Problems with culture and attitudes cannot be addressed by
developing a new policy, changing the rules or developing
a new process.'

Baroness Casey, review into the Metropolitan Police[1]

Before I launch into this chapter about structure, operating models, processes and the like, let me make a statement. Culture does not belong to HR (and here I'm including – for the benefit of ease – all people functions here, whatever they may be called at your organization) in the same way that spending money doesn't belong to finance. While it's easy to say to a HR manager, 'Culture belongs to you', it simply doesn't work that way. Indeed, saying or thinking that can actually generate a toxic culture of its own!

This seems to be lost on most organizations and often when toxic cultures arise, well-meaning recommendations seem to focus solely on upskilling the HR function, rather than recognizing that culture belongs to everyone and therefore everyone needs to be involved in its change, including HR! In fact, in many cases of toxicity, HR has been complicit in either ineffective process or not taking allegations seriously enough.

Take this recommendation from the report into the allegations of toxic culture at the Confederation of British Industry (CBI) in 2023:

Inattention to people and culture function: People and culture/HR has not been prioritized as a core strategic function with sufficient oversight from leaders and the Board.

Or this one following a report into the toxic culture at Prince Edward Island (PEI) University as a result of allegations of bullying, harassment, racism and misogyny:

> *In a statement on June 14, the university said an action plan would be developed based on the report. The statement from Keefe and Sinnott also said the university would install a 'vice-president of people and culture', who would oversee human resources, diversity efforts, sexual violence prevention and response services, and report to the university's president.*[2]

HR has a responsibility for defining process and procedure with regards to reporting and dealing with behaviour and performance. However, it's an inattention from *all* functions – not just HR – that has given rise to allegations of toxicity at both the CBI and PEI University. Any individual or department could have insisted more could have been done, but they didn't. That said, as owners of the process and procedure, HR has a duty to act swiftly and decisively where behaviour or performance doesn't meet the agreed organizational standards. And if I'm being honest, it doesn't always happen.

As I mentioned earlier in Chapter 1: What is toxic culture?, UK morning TV show *This Morning* has also faced allegations of a toxic culture. Speaking publicly about it, former regular guest Dr Ranj Singh said that he'd raised his concerns about a toxic culture over two years previously and not only did nothing ever happen, but they started to use him less and less. He said, 'I even took my concerns directly to the top of ITV: the culture at *This Morning* had become toxic, no longer aligned with ITV values, and I felt like because I whistle-blew, I was managed out.'[3]

ITV, the producers of the show, countered his allegations by saying that they ran an internal investigation and found no evidence to support his claims. That doesn't change the fact, however, that to Ranj, it *felt* toxic. Many senior leaders and HR/People and Culture departments are still struggling with the concept that culture is often a 'feeling' and that such feelings may be different depending on where you work or who you work for.

There was a similar situation at PEI University. A report into the toxic culture allegations found that behaviour from some professors directed at co-workers and students 'carried on for years without being addressed in any meaningful way, despite multiple complaints'.[4] It would ultimately lead to the chair of the board resigning, stating that 'new leadership is required to address the university's problems'.[5]

This is not going to be a 3,500-word HR-blaming chapter (as much as some people would love that!). However, there are three issues at play here:

1. The board/senior leadership team think that having a department that has the word 'culture' in the title means it absolves them (and others) of the responsibility for maintaining a watching brief on working conditions and how people feel within it. But it doesn't.

2. Often HR/People and Culture teams don't understand how cultures are built and maintained and can't provide expert guidance to push through the steps required to address cultural issues in a timely and bold manner.

3. However, even when they do, HR/People and Culture departments don't often have the respect that they deserve when it comes to highlighting cultural issues or requiring support – both financial and time – from senior leaders to invest in addressing them.

The second point may be contentious for HR leaders. However, a client of mine, a head of global HR, spoke at a conference in Europe recently and was staggered by 'the number of my peers who simply don't understand the very thing that they're supposed to be in charge of. They seem to be more concerned about process than people.'

When I wrote my book *Culture Fix*, it was in part a result of this fact, based on the experiences of my own nearly 30-year career as an employee. I wanted to outline in very simple terms just what it takes to create an environment of success as culture continues to be something that people in business talk about, but don't really understand well enough. So, as I get into outlining the structures and processes required to deal with or avoid a toxic culture, it's important to understand that culture is everyone's responsibility and while HR may be the custodian of culture (in the same way that Finance are the custodians of how money spent is reported), they don't own it. However, they will need the full support of the leadership team and middle managers to implement the initiatives they've identified that will enhance the working environment for everyone within it.

Does your structure make sense?

A key part of building a culture to deliver a strategy is ensuring that you have a workforce with the technical and emotional skills to be able to deliver it. And the workforce must be organized in a way that provides equity and leads to effective collaboration between the functions.

The type of structure you need will very much depend on the type of business, its size and locations, as well as how leaders wish to execute the strategy. Often the latter is built on the level of trust or empowerment that exists or else it centres around technical capability. You can't just pluck a structure out of thin air or hope that it grows organically. This will lead to confusion, a bottleneck in decision-making, fiefdoms, land grabs and all manner of toxic behaviour from people looking to exert control over their corner of the organization. The structure – and the processes that support it – need to be intelligently designed and efficiently implemented. And by that, I mean that they need to be simple to understand and the work needs to be easy to do. The best structures allow employees to draw an imaginary line from the work that they do to the ultimate success of the organization without hitting any barriers. Yet according to McKinsey,[6] only 23 per cent of organizational redesigns are implemented effectively, with 44 per cent stalling and 33 per cent failing outright. And when the design of how work gets done – regardless of what it is – isn't effective, then it creates problems everywhere.

Let's take an Olympic team as an example. The overall goal of the team may be linked to medals won or position in the league table as a result. However, it would make no sense at all if the structure had the runners working with the hockey coaches, the pole vaulters working with the marathon coaches, or the chef de mission (posh name for 'leader of an international sports team') as a participating athlete themselves. Athletes and coaches alike would question the structure and outwardly express – to each other and to the media – whether it was set up to deliver success, leading to discontent and – if not dealt with – toxicity. Especially given the amount of work and money required by athletes to compete in the Olympics in the first place.

But the process for designing and implementing a structure needn't be as onerous as many organizations make it. This is not to imply that the discussions and decisions themselves aren't complex, however the process is relatively straightforward:

1. Work with members of the team to understand what an efficient organization needs to look like to achieve the purpose/vision (everything has to tie back to this) and thus deliver on the strategy.
2. Confirm the budget and/or staff numbers available.
3. Consult on a proposed structure, writing down the responsibilities of each team member and the value they can add.
4. Recruit people for the roles that you've identified, establishing whether they have the skills required to complete the role effectively (technical and emotional).
5. Communicate it clearly and set a date by which it will be implemented, so that everyone can move forward together.

Through my research on toxic cultures, lots of time is wasted by senior managers trying to come up with the perfect structural model to deliver value. There are many different models to choose from, all or none of which could be right for your organization.

The Canadian academic and author on business and management Henry Mintzberg is just one of many people to write about such models, having written over 150 articles and 15 books on the topic. However, what I like about Mintzberg's approach is his focus on what happens in the real world, rather than what should work theoretically.

Mintzberg identified six types of organizational configurations, as follows:

1. *Simple*

    This approach is the one adopted by most simple or new organizations. Most start-ups take this approach as there tends to be no formality around the way that work gets done. Work is flexible and fluid and there is little in the way of middle management. Often there's a single leader at the top, making key decisions. Autonomy is high in simple structures.

2. *Machine*

    Such an approach contains lots of standardization, with every step being formal in nature. This generally leads to high levels of specialization and works best for those organizations (such as government departments) that are highly regulated or that require work to be completed in a particular way. Middle managers are required to check that work has been completed in the 'right' way.

3. *Professional*

    This approach shares much with the machine bureaucracy, especially around the formal nature of work and the standardization of inputs. However, unlike the machine approach, employees in this structure are highly skilled and have much higher degrees of autonomy, meaning that decision-making power is spread across the organization. Accounting companies, consulting companies and lawyers tend to use this approach.

4. *Diversified*

   The approach requires a head office to coordinate with divisions on how work gets done. Unlike the machine structure, middle managers are provided with more autonomy on how work gets done in their part of the organization, with the central team providing the mechanics to support this. This approach is adopted by large global businesses or manufacturing companies that produce a range of products.

5. *Adhocracy*

   This approach is characterized by its focus on continual creativity and innovation. As the name suggests, there is little formality nor any respect shown for the way that other, more established organizations operate. The emphasis is on employees within this structure to work together as required to achieve goals. There are lots of managers in this approach that focus on unique projects. Amazon has long been cited as an example of an adhocracy.

6. *Missionary*

   This approach relies on its employees to agree on a set of core beliefs. It is the beliefs that unite people – regardless of how the organization is itself structured – and drive commitment to the work. Small, loosely organized units work together in pursuit of a distinctive mission. This approach is often favoured by religious groups.

Each of these approaches are supported by what Mintzberg called the ideology – i.e. the beliefs, values and norms of the way that work gets done, i.e. the culture.

Each of these approaches can be highly efficient, depending on the nature of business, the strategic goals and the social culture within which it operates. However, each approach can also generate toxicity. Common signs for each approach are as follows:

1. *Simple*
   - Micro-management

- Decision bottleneck
- Perfectionism

2. *Machine*
    - Command and control
    - Bureaucracy
    - Risk-averse

3. *Professional*
    - Internal competition
    - Compromised values
    - Unethical behaviour

4. *Diversified*
    - Siloes
    - Interdepartmental conflict
    - Unclear priorities

5. *Adhocracy*
    - Lack of direction
    - Compromised quality
    - No clear accountability

6. *Missionary*
    - Leadership built on charisma
    - Alienation of those with differing viewpoints
    - Misuse of resources.

The Confederation of British Industry (CBI) is a not-for-profit organization that represents the interests of its clients (UK businesses and trade associations) at the highest levels of government. In the 2023 report into its toxic culture, an inconsistent structure was just one of the issues found by those reviewing it. It was stated, 'There is a lack of clear or consistent structures and processes for decision making. Activities are driven by the priorities of the Director General, with deep organizational siloes.'

Interestingly (and referring back to my point earlier), one of the ways that the CBI is addressing this – outlined in their prospectus, *A Renewed CBI* – is the creation of a new People and Culture subcommittee. Sigh.

Nintendo US was another company that faced toxic allegations around its structure in 2022. In a special investigation conducted by news outlet IGN, they found – through interviewing current and former staff – practices that involved deliberately excluding contract staff from team activities, enforcing strict attendance policies and even terminating temporary workers for attending funerals of close family members.[8] The separation between contract and permanent employees, is something which I discuss more in Chapter 7, Does empathy exist?.

Are your processes preventing action on toxicity?

Regardless of which approach your organization takes to structure itself, there is still a certain amount of process required to ensure that you successfully guard against the risk of toxicity or support people who wish to address it quickly so that it doesn't spread. And my own experiences of these processes as a manager for 20 years weren't that great.

This is something that social psychologist Tessa West talked about in 2022 in an interview with *HR Director* magazine, saying, 'The business of handling complaints by HR specialists is often a wait-and-see one: wait until the grievances come in, and then they come up with a plan of action.'[9] Or worse, take no action at all.

The Baroness Casey Review[10] into the toxic culture at the Metropolitan Police in the UK in 2023 brought to light many horrific things that people hope never to witness in their working lives. Bullying, harassment, misogyny and institutional racism were all cited in the 363-page report. I read many of these kinds of reports to better understand what is happening in different workplaces around the world, in order to better inform my work, yet I have never read anything so harrowing and upsetting as this one.

Disappointingly, many of the findings are simply a repeat of previous reviews of the culture undertaken at various stages over the last 40 years. They were known problems that were never dealt with in a meaningful way that would bring about a change in the organization's culture. The fact that the issues still exist is a complete and utter failure of senior management and government officials over four decades.

It's extremely difficult to distil the review down into key themes, yet one thing was evident throughout that I believe you can learn from to ensure you avoid the toxicity – and ensuing publicity – wrought upon the Met. And that is, that leaders and the processes employed by the organization actively discouraged people from speaking up about what they'd seen or heard: 'There is a culture of not speaking out in the Met. Leaders merely exhorting people to "speak up" will not change this culture while people's experience of doing so remains so negative.'

A similar issue was raised by political advisor Sue Gray as part of the investigation into Partygate,[11] the scandal that led to the removal of Boris Johnson as UK Prime Minister. In her report, she said, 'some staff had witnessed or been subjected to behaviours at work which they had felt concerned about but at times felt unable to raise properly'. It would be easy to think that this is specific just to the Met or the UK Government, however, it also happens in other workplaces around the world.

So, why is it important to build processes that encourage a 'speak-up' culture?

The positives of a 'speak-up' culture

Principally, when employees are able to share their ideas, concerns and feedback openly, it can lead to a more positive and productive culture, which in turn not only enhances the employee experience, but also the experience of stakeholders or customers working with them. However, it's also a way to spot early warning signs of toxic culture developing, either through the behaviour of people, inefficient working practices, excessive workloads or misuse of technology, to name but four reasons.

The last thing that you want to do – which is the reality for many – is to find out about the kind of culture that you have via the news.

Here's how building a 'speak-up' culture positively affects day-to-day activity:

- **Immediate action:** In situations where poor behaviour is observed, employees are more likely to escalate these to management, who can take immediate action to address them and thus prevent the culture from becoming toxic.
- **Engagement:** When employees feel heard and valued, they are more engaged in their work and invested in the achievement of goals (personal and team).
- **Loyalty:** Employees who feel they are listened to are more likely to stay with the organization long-term.
- **Belonging:** When employees are able to talk freely and openly about behaviour and performance, it increases the bonds they feel towards those that they work with and the culture as a whole.
- **Trust:** If employees feel that they not only have permission to speak up, but also that something will be done with the feedback they provide, it will increase the trust between managers and employees.
- **Innovation:** Employees who are able to speak up are more likely to share new and innovative ideas, which can drive growth and progress within the company.
- **Problem solving:** When employees feel comfortable speaking up, they are more likely to raise issues or concerns before they become bigger problems. This can help the company to address issues more quickly and effectively.

To help employees feel more comfortable speaking up in the workplace, I would recommend the following steps:

1. Build a culture of open, two-way communication: Leaders should create an environment where open communication is encouraged

and valued. This can be done through regular team meetings where feedback is on the agenda, one-on-one check-ins or anonymous suggestion boxes. It's always better to encourage conversation before you send people down the process route.

2. Provide training: Many employees may not feel comfortable speaking up because they lack the communication skills or confidence to do so. By providing training on effective communication and active listening, you can help employees feel more comfortable sharing their thoughts and ideas, but they also need to understand what the process is for doing so.

3. Have an efficient process to capture feedback: running alongside (not instead of) the first two suggestions. You need a simple process for people to provide feedback on what they've seen and provide guidelines on what they can expect and when, should they do so. Having a process isn't enough, those monitoring it need to respond empathetically, quickly and efficiently.

4. Investigate allegations thoroughly: When employees show courage and speak up on issues of ethics or poor behaviour, it's important that their feedback is dealt with empathetically, quickly and efficiently. More serious allegations should be handled by external organizations to ensure that there is no 'whitewashing' of the findings, should senior managers be implicated.

5. Act decisively: Once a thorough investigation has been undertaken, leaders should move decisively to address the issues. HR should be given full autonomy to take whatever action they deem to be necessary to ensure that appropriate action is taken – or feedback provided – to ensure that people feel listened to and the culture safeguarded from future risk of toxic behaviour.

I can't stress enough how important these last two steps are. As I said earlier, it's not enough just to have a process to capture feedback. It's critically important that this feedback is taken seriously and that no stone is unturned in ensuring that people's complaints are thoroughly investigated.

This is not something that Michigan State University did when graduate Amanda Thomashow complained about former gymnastics coach Larry Nassar in 2014. Nassar was eventually convicted in January 2018 of the sexual assault of over 150 women and girls and sentenced to 40–175 years in prison and yet, had the university taken Thomashow's complaint about her treatment at the hands of Nassar seriously in 2014, many of those cases might have been avoided and seen justice brought much earlier. Instead, their Title IX office, which investigates claims around gender discrimination, sexual assault and harassment, thanked her for bringing it to their attention but found that 'she didn't understand the nuanced difference between sexual assault and an appropriate medical procedure'.[12]

But it wasn't the first time that the University had faced allegations of abhorrent behaviour on campus and chosen to do nothing about it. The US Department of Education investigated allegations made against the University and found that 'Many of MSU's case files lacked key documentation, including whether any assistance was offered to those who made allegations and whether MSU took any steps after an investigation to prevent a recurrence of the harassment.'[13]

Managers around the world should take heed of these cases. It would be all too easy to dismiss the findings as being specific to the work that these organizations do, or on a scale that's unimaginable for you. Almost every organization beset by toxic culture allegations at some stage probably thought, 'that could never happen here'. However, without building a culture that values and welcomes employees who speak up and then thoroughly investigates any allegations made, any organization could find itself in a similar position.

An operating model that doesn't operate

The colloquial term used to describe the strategy, structure and processes employed by an organization is 'Operating Model'. Senior managers love to talk about operating models as there is still a misplaced perception that if you get the structure and processes right, then the culture will magically take care of itself, which of course it never does. In fact, changes to the operating model often make the situation worse and lead to a toxic culture themselves. Employees will see senior leaders changing elements of the business that don't affect the root cause of problems that are undermining performance.

The restructure is a perfect example of this. Recently, I worked with a team in the UK who had a perfectly pleasant culture, one where people were nice to each other. Performance, however, was nowhere near where it needed to be and three high potential employees had left. The manager had waited to run the culture workshop until after a planned restructure had been completed. Prior to spending three days with the team, we ran a short survey to better understand the root causes of why the culture wasn't vibrant. The greatest number of comments centred on the recent restructure. Here's a sample of them:

- 'The restructure has led to confusion and I feel we've fallen back even further from where we were'
- 'The restructure wasn't required as much as managing out two poorly behaving individuals was. They're still here'
- 'I really don't understand why the structure has changed. Communication has been poor and this contributed to the resignations of key people'
- 'We are just shuffling deckchairs on the *Titanic*.'

Naturally, a culture survey isn't complete without a reference to the seating arrangements on a centuries-old vessel which now resides at the bottom of the Atlantic Ocean! Still, you can't help but feel for these employees, who simply want to understand why the decision to change the structure was taken, rather than dealing with the root cause issues. Through the survey we identified these root causes as:

1. Two poorly behaving managers
2. Unrealistic workload expectations
3. Unclear priorities
4. Disconnected senior leadership team
5. Poor use of technology.

Incidentally, these issues were also raised through the organization's own engagement survey (see Chapter 10: How will you respond? for more on this topic), yet a restructure was seen as the answer, rather than the more difficult tasks of performance management, reprioritization of work and some basic agreements on how people should work together.

The inquiry into the toxic culture at the Metropolitan Police Service in the UK is one that I will refer to a number of times throughout this book. In short, a litany of leadership failures contributed to a culture where police officers treated each other and the general public horrifically. Met chief Sir Mark Rowley QPM was appointed to address the findings of the Casey Review and key to the success of this work is to start by removing those employees whose conduct has fallen short of what's expected. Removal of toxic people is key to being able to reset the culture, so in this scenario this is the right place to start. Yet, what he's already found is that the 'machine' that sits behind how the Met is run – the processes, structures and governance – doesn't allow him to take the action that he needs to take. When quizzed on the changes he's looking to make, he expressed his frustrations: 'Some of the decisions are made outside the Met, so people we've decided shouldn't be police officers, an independent lawyer says "bad luck, you've got to keep them". That can't be right. No other employer has to deal with that.'

Rowley also said that he needs 'changes in regulations to help me get on with them because some of the processes are too long and too bureaucratic.'

Bureaucracy is the practice whereby organizations decide to make it hard for themselves to get work done. Please don't confuse this with legislation that has to be followed in order for organizations to satisfy regulators that they're doing the right things. Bureaucracy is the art of making work harder than it needs to be and is often presided over by micro-managers or else individuals are invested in keeping things exactly the way they are.

In bureaucratic organizations you will hear phrases such as:

- Rules are rules.
- It *has* to be done that way.
- It makes no sense to anyone, but that's the process.

Research from Aiken and Hage in 1966[14] found that companies that instigate formal bureaucratic processes are more likely to generate alienation between individuals and to the work that they do. This was especially prevalent as an organization grows. The researchers acknowledged that conflicts and power dynamics are inherent in bureaucratic organizations. As different units and individuals compete for people, resources and influence, conflicts may arise as decision-making becomes more centralized.

This was an issue faced in 2019 by Amnesty International, which was found to have contributed to a toxic culture where two employees killed themselves. The KonTerra Report[15] into the culture found, 'significant risk of experiencing secondary stress or vicarious trauma as a result of the work being undertaken' and that the organization was operating in a 'state of emergency' following a restructure that had moved staff closer to places of conflict and unrest.[16]

In bureaucratic organizations, power struggles or restructures can impact decision-making processes and the overall functioning of the culture, leading to combatant relationships between teams and ultimately, toxicity as the battles become all-out wars. As the KonTerra Report stated, 'Amnesty International cannot effectively strive to make the world a better place while perpetuating an organizational culture deeply marked by secrecy, mistrust, nepotism and other forms of power abuse.'

Bureaucracy or changes to the operating model more generally needn't be the enemy of growth. It's possible to positively evolve the culture in a way that doesn't increase the need for confusion, micro-management, personality clashes or more process or paperwork. This requires that a proactive approach is taken to operating model assessment and the cultural evolution required to ensure that results are achieved. Put simply, there has to be a compelling reason for setting up an organization in the way that you want it, which is understandable by all. This understanding will provide the clarity required for culture definition.

As McKinsey said in their State of Organizations report in 2023, '*The CEO will need to present a compelling case for the changes being proposed and a detailed overview of their implications across the organization.*' The report continues, '*If senior leaders agree with the case, the CEO can begin to create a blueprint for the new operating model, taking a system view of the operating model and then determining how to rewire its parts rather than considering piecemeal changes.*' [17]

The rewiring described above will always impact the culture negatively, if not handled in the right way. However, even if it is handled responsibly, the culture will still need to be reset to ensure that the sense of belonging is refreshed to the new operating model.

The longer you wait to make operating model changes, the greater the chances that the culture will turn toxic. Deciding on the changes is the easy bit; executing them, while maintaining employee excitement for the impending cultural evolution, is quite different and will require excellent communication – and a growth mindset around what's possible – from all involved.

The components of the operating model and the culture required to deliver it are highly intertwined, which is why, in order to avoid any kind of toxicity, each is treated with equal importance.

Detox your culture: actions

It is possible to have a vibrant culture without any kind of structure at all. For start-ups, this initially feels liberating, particularly if they previously operated within a corporate environment. Yet as the organization grows, it's crucial that the operating model scales with it.

It's simply not possible to retain the structure and processes of a 10-person business in a 50- to 100-person one. The operating model needs to be fit for purpose in order that staff can create the culture required to help the organization to achieve its goals. While the onus is largely on the HR/People department to do this, everyone has a role in ensuring that their part of the organization scales accordingly and does so equitably.

By consistently challenging the way that work gets done, organizations can ensure that continual improvement is built into the culture, rather than it being a goal that they aspire to and by allowing employees to do this regularly, the chances of toxic culture are reduced.

Five things:

1. Ensure that your HR/People function is given the teeth it requires to safeguard the culture.
2. Build a structure that encourages information sharing and collaboration.
3. Ensure that processes make it easy to report toxic culture and to get work done.
4. Implement a 'speak-up' process to provide you with early warnings of potential toxicity.
5. Continually evolve the operating model (and culture) to ensure that it remains fit for purpose.

CHAPTER FIVE

What do you value?

'We have the power, by living the values, to build the culture.
We also have the power, by breaking the values, to fuck
up the culture.'

Brian Chesky – Founder, AirBnB

What do Enron, Wells Fargo, Volkswagen, *The Ellen Show* and the Minneapolis Police Department all have in common?

Answer: They all proclaimed values that they failed to live up to in practice.

Enron had a value of 'integrity' yet deliberately deceived regulators by hiding mountains of debt and assets.[1] The company went bankrupt in 2021 and many of its senior managers served time in jail. Founder Kenneth Lay died of a heart attack prior to his sentencing.[2]

Wells Fargo[3] had a value of 'ethics' yet its employees created millions of accounts for customers in order to meet sales targets and those that phoned the ethics hotline to report this practice were fired.[4]

Volkswagen had values of 'renewability', 'respect', 'responsibility' and 'sustainability' yet it was found that in order to meet environmental standards around diesel fuel emissions, Volkswagen had modified the software on over 11m cars to falsify carbon dioxide emission levels.[5] Oh, and the leadership initially lied about doing this, only admitting it once they were presented with evidence. They were fined a total of c.US$30bn.[6]

The Ellen Show[7] was built on the value of 'Be Kind', yet employees made public allegations of fear, racism, misconduct and intimidation, leading to a public apology from the host: 'Things happened here that should never have happened.'[8]

Finally, and most significantly, the Minneapolis Police Department had values of 'Trust', 'Accountability' and 'Professional Service' yet this did not stop Officer Derek Chauvin from kneeling on George Floyd's neck for nine minutes and 29 seconds, leading to Floyd's death and sparking global outrage.[9]

To be honest, I could fill this entire chapter with global case studies of companies that professed a set of 'values' but then chose (and it is a choice, after all) not to practise them, leading to the development of a toxic culture. The decision not to live the values ultimately had a significant impact on the lives of humans, financial penalties, jail time and irreparable reputational damage. All because they said one thing, then did another. And before you tell yourself that it will never happen at your organization, answer this question: 'How can you be so sure?'

The true value of values

When your organization has a set of well-written values and they are seen to be practised by all staff, employees have been found to be 115 per cent more engaged. Greater engagement leads to greater productivity, improved loyalty, better customer service, improved results and so on. Done well, values can change everything.[10] The fact is though that most companies don't do them well. In fact, the same survey found that only 33 per cent of employees believed that their managers held their staff accountable to their values.

Around 80 per cent of the Fortune 100 companies have their values (also called things like 'principles', 'beliefs', 'mantras' and so on) on their websites. Many of these companies even spend hundreds of thousands of dollars creating them and marketing them.[11] Yet if staff aren't engaged in the process of defining them, they're badly written or they're ignored in times of crisis, then they're worthless.

MIT Sloan research found that 75 per cent of the 500 companies that they surveyed had a list of core values, but that the 'correlation coefficient between how heavily a company weighted a set of values and how well employees said they did on those specific values hovered around zero'.[12]

In times of crisis or uncertainty it's the values demonstrated by its people that determine whether a culture will embrace change or turn toxic. I spoke to an employee recently whose organization has values of 'Evolution' and 'Brilliant People' and yet they pulled all staff and culture development funding for the next financial year. This is an example of a culture that is values-*written*, not values-*driven*.

A values-driven culture would be creative about the way they develop their staff next year. Cancelling needless travel, pointless projects or reducing the number of external people they hire in order to double down on the evolution of the business through the development of the brilliant people that they already have.

But what does it actually mean to be values-driven?

Values are not single words used to tick a culture box. They are statements that the organization (and its culture) hold to be true and are, in effect, an agreement on how humans will interact with each other on a daily basis.

When an organization is values-driven, they don't talk about these values – instead they actively bring them to life in everything that they do. They are used to inform decisions around customer interactions, projects to be undertaken, how to treat staff and how to safeguard the planet for the next generation; they are also used for hiring. Organizations that are values-driven only hire people who believe the same things they do and all of those checks are done before adding someone to the payroll – all of which may take more than three interviews.

For values-driven organizations, hiring isn't about finding someone with a pulse to do immediate work, it's about finding a person who can contribute to the culture in a way that enhances belonging and performance. Unfortunately, one survey found that only one in five of employees feels that their organization always hires people that fit their values.[13]

In order to avoid toxicity and build a workforce that's fit for the future, it's critically important to do this exercise well. Nearly two in five Gen Z and Millennial employees have rejected a job or assignment because of values misalignment. Indeed, if an organization doesn't act in the way that it says it will, 35 per cent of Gen Z and Millennials will walk away *without* another job to go to![14]

The average tenure for Millennial and Gen Z employees – who will make up almost 75 per cent of the workforce in 2030[15] – is currently 2.9 years. Yet when an organization takes the time to build a strong culture which values societal and environmental issues, they are more likely to stay for over five years. And to be clear, it's not just about stating a value of 'We love the planet', it's about reducing carbon footprint, using energy-efficient office space and not printing out mountains of emails and reports.[16] Fundamentally, values are about the treatment of humans, by the organization and by each other.

I read a story in June 2023 about a group of UK businesses[17] who had been fined for not paying their people enough. One of the organizations was the high-street retailer WHSmith. A spokesperson said, 'This was a genuine error and it was rectified immediately with all colleagues reimbursed.' Funnily enough, one of their values (at time of writing) is 'Value our People'.

My question here would be, what checks were in place to ensure that you truly value your people by paying them for the hours that they work? I'm fairly certain that no such mistakes are made when pricing products in order to make profits (in 2022, WH Smith profits totalled £73mn).

It wasn't just them, of course. Retailer Marks & Spencer was also fined in 2023. Their spokesperson said, 'This happened simply because temporary colleagues were not paid within the strict time periods specified in the national minimum wage regulations and was remedied as soon as we became aware of the issue.'

Note here, not only was it *simple* (try telling that to those who were underpaid) but M&S also had to be made aware of this issue – they weren't checking that they'd paid people properly. And yet, one of their values is 'trust'. This from their 2023 Annual Report, 'Since its inception, M&S has built trust by doing the right thing by its people and the communities it serves, and this remains one of its core values today'.[18] Indeed…

With a Glassdoor score of 3.7 (out of a possible 5), it's clear that M&S still has some work to do. You can't tell the world that you have a values-based culture, the people you employ will do it for you. Or else, they'll bring it into the public domain or sue you.

As I mentioned earlier in this chapter, values provide emotional direction and have to be specific to what the organization and its people believe. Researchers Graham, Harvey, Poadek and Rajgopal characterize them as 'ideals employees strive to fulfil'.[19] Values inform behaviour and when coupled with the norms of how work gets done (see Chapter 8: How does work get done?), you have an agreement on how the strategy will be delivered.

Values often get confused with the things that the organization should be doing by default and exhibit A is diversity and inclusion. Diversity and inclusion (D&I) isn't a value or a policy, it is the way that the organization structures itself and acts in its everyday business operations and how it hires, to address the gaps that it has in the way that it thinks. This is not an easy thing to do. After all, if every organization was already diverse and inclusive, they wouldn't be spending thousands on re-educating people on what it means or making grand statements about it on their website or in their annual reports.

Diversity is about building a workforce that not only represents the social environment in which the company operates, but also the people it serves. This includes race, ethnicity, gender and cognition (i.e. how different people think). It also includes faith, political and social differences.

Inclusion is about ensuring that all employees have an equal voice and are listened to. In many respects this will be the demonstration of whether diversity is taken seriously or not. For example, if the same loud white male voices, who are paid more than their female counterparts, continue to dominate decision-making then all efforts to create an equitable environment that promotes difference will be lost. Organizations that truly value diversity and inclusion will generate fairness in all of their operations. They see improvement across almost all business result areas and create loyalty and belonging throughout their workforce.

In a recent report[20] from Employee Engagement Tool company CultureAmp, it was found that 74 per cent of those surveyed said that senior leaders in their organization supported D&I efforts, but that only 34 per cent said that they had sufficient resources to do this work. The same report also found that women feel less supported and less able to take a break than men do; that people of colour don't feel like they have the opportunities as white employees and also, they don't feel that their opinions are as valued.

Another piece of research found that over a third of respondents reported their company simply wasn't doing enough to address discrimination. D&I programs that employees perceive to be ineffective 'result in a 78 per cent decrease in engagement, a 66 per cent decrease in the perception of the employee experience, and a 44 per cent increase in moderate to severe burnout'.[21]

What that means is that lip service is still being paid to D&I in many organizations around the world. Having a policy is one thing, having tangible metrics that demonstrate that you're delivering on the policy is something else. With the latter comes accountability for the senior leadership team, which is where ultimate responsibility lies for ensuring that an organization is doing all it can to build a workforce to serve its diverse customer base.

Hiring and tracking employees

There's also an emerging problem – linked to hiring by values – when it comes to ensuring that you have a diverse workforce and that is, the rise of recruitment by artificial intelligence (AI). At the time of writing, the world is in somewhat of a panic over AI (which I talk about in more detail in Chapter 9: Are you standing still?), which may or may not be justified and may or may not be linked to what people have seen in the movies. 'It's going to be like *2001: A Space Odyssey/Blade Runner/Robocop/Terminator/The Matrix/Mission Impossible*! [Delete as appropriate for you].' Although, never about *Short Circuit* or *Brian and Charles* for some reason?

According to Ian Siegel, CEO of ZipRecruiter, at least three quarters of all resumes for vacant roles submitted to organizations in the US are read by algorithms. When interviewed, he said, 'The dawn of robot recruiting has come and went, and people just haven't caught up to the realization yet.'[22]

While organizations should continually experiment with technology to ensure that it improves the way that they do things, they also have to ensure that it doesn't compromise the culture that they need to build to support the delivery of products and services. In the case of using algorithms for recruiting, organizations need to ensure (or be assured by the companies selling these tools), that the technology will lead to fairer employment practices.

No global standards currently exist around algorithmic hiring (which is true of most AI practices at time of writing). However, given that 55 per cent of HR leaders in the US alone now use them – whether it's for candidate selection or interview transcription, for example – it's incumbent upon each to ensure that no bias exists.

Unfortunately, research shows that it does. The Brookings Institute audited employment algorithms and found that some models that used language demonstrated bias against women and people with disabilities. Speech recognition tools demonstrated bias against African-Americans and 'Algorithms that disseminate job postings can unintentionally result in biased outcomes against young women for STEM jobs and similarly ageism against older candidates.'[23] Given that in the US, 47 per cent of black people see racial bias as an issue during the hiring process, it's clear that organizations need to safeguard them against this. Oh, and one final thing: If you truly value your workforce, you won't track them, ever.

If there's one thing the pandemic accelerated, it was a move to greater use of technology. The barriers and fixed mindsets to the use of technology have now been removed and tools are being used in ways that many businesses never thought possible. However, leaders should not abuse this and use it for ill will. At the time of writing, sales of employee tracking tools have risen by as much as 300 per cent,[24] so many have already implemented it. However, tracking the movements of employees (unless necessary for the job, e.g. emergency services) is an insidious practice that merely demonstrates that senior managers have absolutely no trust in their employees whatsoever. And let's be honest here, employees are smart enough to find a way around it anyway.[25]

This issue is being actively addressed by the US government[26] after a report in the *New York Times*[27] found that eight of the 10 largest private companies tracked workers to assess their productivity. Microsoft – an organization that provides tools to track employees – found, in its own research, that 85 per cent of managers[28] have trouble believing that their employees are being productive. Which, of course, says more about the skillsets of managers in setting and holding people to expectations and the ability to trust humans to do the right thing than it does about the level of work getting done.

This is an issue where I feel we're just scratching the surface of. However, make no mistake: not only will tracking the productivity of workers lead to them leaving the organization (in one survey, over half of respondents said they would quit rather than be tracked),[29] it will also lead to a backlash, unwanted news coverage and thus an inability to attract high-potential employees to safeguard business success.

Values done well

Zappos is an online shoe retailer based in Las Vegas in the US. It was founded by Nick Swinmurn, Alfred Lin and (the late) Tony Hsieh – the latter of whom was to become its figurehead – in 1999. They had a rapid rise and in 2008 appeared on the Fortune Top 100 Companies to Work For list, something that Hsieh was incredibly proud of and sought to maintain through a commitment to great culture. And at the heart of that culture are 10 core values, the practice of which contribute to their continued success. As stated on their website, 'Our 10 core values are more than just words. They're a way of life.'[30]

The use of these values starts before a person is even hired. During the recruitment process, they go to great lengths to ensure that people are a good values fit. They recognize that they'll only grow as a business if they hire people who understand what it means to live their 10 core values in pursuit of their purpose, 'To live and deliver WOW'.

A person's skills and potential will get them an interview at Zappos and the first interview will be conducted by the potential line manager of the role. The second interview, however, is conducted by an independent person within the organization who can assess whether the candidate is a good values-match for the organization.

Zappos' values – like many organizations who do this exercise well – are visible everywhere. Staff identity badges, merchandise, walls around the office but most importantly, in the behaviours of their employees. The values are seen as sacrosanct, something that Hsieh wrote about in his book, *Delivering Happiness: Profits, Passion and*

Purpose. He says, 'There are plenty of examples of companies with a lot more money that have gone out of business because they became careless or overconfident, celebrating their past successes instead of carefully navigating for the future.'[31]

In 2019, I spent three days at their headquarters in Las Vegas and gained some fascinating cultural insights into how they put their values into practice. I also learned about 'The Offer'.

Hsieh pioneered this 'get paid to quit' scheme as a way of safeguarding the culture at the end of a new employee's induction period. In his view, four weeks was a long enough time for both the organization and the new employee to assess whether they were a good values-match. Those that obviously weren't didn't have their contracts confirmed and left the organization, while those that management felt were a good fit were still offered USD$2000 to leave. Hsieh felt this was a better alternative to having to manage them out at a later date when they didn't embody what the organization stood for.

While in Vegas, I also asked Hsieh what happens when money is tight as I was interested in whether – like many other organizations – spending money on culture was pulled when targets hadn't been hit. He said: '[in times of financial issues] we always cut the culture stuff last.' His assertion was that by removing money to work on the culture, you run the risk of compromising talent development and breaking the machine that produces the results. This is what it means to be values-driven and the complete opposite of what most organizations would do. However, values (like most things in the world of workplace culture) aren't forever.

Despite my excitement at meeting Tony Hsieh, I also wanted to ask him a difficult question, so I did.

Me: 'Tony, the organization has strong values and it's great to see them
 lived in plain sight. My question is: how often do you change them?'
Tony: 'Our values will always be our values. They won't change.'

It's hard to disagree with someone who had a great track record in building successful culture, but on this issue I did – and still do – disagree. Like everything in workplace cultures, values can never be a 'set and forget' exercise. As the business grows, as the world changes, as employees' views evolve, then the values must do likewise.

Granted, values don't change every year as a vision statement could, but they can never be the same values forever. That would be to admit that nothing within the company would ever change. In that scenario the values will simply stop being lived, because they don't mean anything to anyone anymore or else are seen as being old, tired or just not relevant.

This is something acknowledged by Google. They call their values 'Ten things we know to be true', which form part of their Philosophy. Under the heading on their webpage they state quite clearly, 'From time to time we revisit this list to see if it still holds true. We hope it does – and you can hold us to that.'[32]

Here are four examples of values exercises that I ran in 2023 and how they speak to the evolution of values. One or more of these scenarios could be true for you too:

- **One for a newly merged company:** This organization recognized that in bringing two companies together, they needed both sets of employees to work together to define a new set of values. The goal was to ensure that there was an appreciation of the work done in the previous two organizations, but that a new set of emotional principles was designed to inform a more joined-up way of working.
- **One for a company that recently acquired two new businesses:** This organization wanted to ensure that the current values that they have also embody the expanded business and its new employees. We'd done some work on values prior to them acquiring the new businesses. However, what we wanted to do here was to not only get feedback from the new members of the team on their values and how they'd been used, but also

to talk about the work that we'd done and how the values were used at this organization.

- **One for a national arm of a global organization:** Values, along with vision and purpose, are the things within the workplace culture that are defined by a global headquarters. However, how they're applied day-to-day may differ from country to country. I worked with an Asian organization who had a presence in 10 countries and I helped each country to understand how they would be applied to each.

- **One, because, well, their current values are a bit rubbish:** This organization recognized that the exercise they undertook many years ago no longer hits the mark for the people that they're looking to employ, now and in the future. Their values were composed of just single words, which in reality described a behaviour, not a value, leaving people confused. Therefore, we pulled a group of people together from across the organization to redesign values that were contemporary and fit for purpose.

The UK's HMRC (His Majesty's Revenue and Customs) department made the news in 2019 after it published a report that found that, among other things, there was a clear gap between the stated values of the organization and 'the real experiences on the ground'. At the time they had four values of respect, professionalism, innovation and integrity; none of which are actual values per se. Three are behaviours (respectful, professional and innovative) and integrity is something you gain by living by values – it can't be a value in and of itself.

Anyway, that glaring aberration aside, feedback from staff was pretty damning and included this comment, 'A dehumanizing work environment for colleagues working in contact centre environments was described extensively.' Which is the antithesis of the four values. More on the details of this review later. However, once the dust had settled, HMRC relaunched new values, which was absolutely required, given that the previous ones weren't adhered to. The new values are as follows:

- We are professional
- We act with integrity
- We show respect
- We are innovative.

Notice any similarities?

To give them their due they are now worded to read more like values (one tick for that), but they are, in fact, exactly the same words, thus proving that nothing has really changed at HMRC. Expect another report in a few years' time that will show that things have got worse. Maybe they could reorder the values or add the word 'still' to each?

When you spend time getting the values right (and many businesses do it really well), it provides managers and employees with the information to translate them into cultural norms. These are then upheld through the behaviours of staff to create efficient ways to work together, where a sense of belonging exists alongside a desire to do well.

Can you have too much culture stuff?

Of course, while not having things such as purpose, vision and values in place or not living them in day-to-day interactions can give rise to a toxic culture, there's also a possibility that organizations can confuse people – and thus give rise to frustration – by having too much culture 'stuff'. By 'stuff' I don't wish to denigrate the good work that organizations do to define the how of work, it's just that often they read in the *Harvard Business Review* about the foundations that all great organizations should have, then organize a leadership away day to agree what these should be. Err, no!

Workplaces are full of well-meaning leaders who define cultural elements that are intended to build a sense of connection and belonging among staff and create the conditions for continual success. But how much is too much? It's a question I'm often asked as many employees are confused about the internal messaging around culture and the expectations around 'consistency of approach'.

I deliberately used the word 'well-meaning' at the start of this piece as I like to believe that many senior leaders recognize the importance of culture and want to create the foundations for success. That said, 'meaning' only becomes 'performance' through practical application and that's where many organizations are found wanting.

Does the purpose describe how the organization wishes to be seen? Is the vision achievable, easy to remember and does the strategy outline how you'll get there? And, have the values been created by employees and do they objectively summarize the kind of behaviours that they want to see (aligned to the purpose and vision)? As I've mentioned, all too often, these exercises are undertaken to 'tick boxes' or as marketing exercises rather than being seen as meaningful pillars of culture.

To avoid confusing employees, leaders and HR departments need to ensure that these pillars are defined, but not go into the detail of how they are actually applied. An overly prescriptive culture leaves managers with no work to do and can lead to confusion, disengagement, toxicity and therefore, an erosion of the belonging that they're looking to create.

When told what the culture is, managers will simply wait for others to take action rather than taking accountability for defining what it means for their own team to live these pillars day-to-day. Ownership and definition of culture requires that managers are provided with the skills to turn good intention into good action. In a webinar that I ran in 2023, over half of the attendees said that this was an area that required further development, which goes some way towards explaining why organizations feel they have to produce thousands of words to describe something that they expect managers to uphold.

By shifting the focus to providing managers with the skills to define how purpose, vision and values will be lived within their own teams, not only will they create cultural ownership across the organization, they will also remove the risk of silos (i.e. where teams can't work well with each other) and thus create the conditions for success. Anything else could lead to culture confusion or worse, toxicity, which will always be a barrier to belonging and, ultimately, performance. And that's a very bad thing.

Another trap that some companies fall into that can lead to a toxic culture is thinking that they can simply come up with some flashy slogans, a new name, some new fonts, a modern logo or write effusively on their website about 'diversity and inclusion efforts' or the like in the hope that people don't scratch below the surface and discover that the culture doesn't match the brand image they wish to portray. This issue was best illustrated by the Bureau of Meteorology in Australia. In October 2022, it released a statement, out of the blue, saying that it wanted to be referred to as *The Bureau* as it was, seemingly, sick of being called the 'BoM'.

Even The Bureau – who are Australia's national weather, climate and water agency – could not have forecasted what happened next. Two days later, enraged by the perceived window dressing taking place, employees and unions contacted government ministers 'alleging bullying, widespread underpayment of overtime for staff, unsafe working hours and a lack of fatigue management'.[33] It further transpired that one employee twice underwent treatment for psychiatric care, while another suffered a heart attack due to excessive overtime work. Additionally, at least five other employees took stress leave, experiencing panic attacks and anxiety.

All of which came to light as a result of a rebranding exercise.

Marketing guru Seth Godin says that brand is 'a promise to people, they have expectations, it's a shorthand, what should I expect the next time'. In this respect, the brand is outward-facing. It's centred on a product (or products), uses stories and imagery to drive customer advocacy and creates a unique selling proposition (USP). Culture, on the other hand, is inward-facing. It's centred on the environment required to build and deliver the products. The environment consists of the values, behaviours, intentions and skills required of employees such that targets can be achieved.

Energy drink company Red Bull is an example of an organization that does both really well and showcases how the two are linked. It has a really strong brand, whose slogan is to 'Give Wiiings to People and Ideas'. If you attend a Red Bull event, you'll see the brand at the heart of everything that they do. They stand for creativity, innovation, confidence and individualism. There's also a really vibrant culture behind the brand, built on strong values. Not only do staff practise the values in plain sight, but they also embody the brand too.

The values at Red Bull were instilled by its founder, the late Dietrich Mateschitz. When asked about the intersection between the brand and its commitment to culture back in 2012, he said, 'the brand is supporting the culture community, as well as the other way round'.[34]

In order to develop a powerful brand you need to build a culture of people who believe in it, then provide them with the freedom to build and evolve it. What you can't do – otherwise you'll be in the news almost daily – is to paint an unrealistic picture of your culture to the outside world in the hope that nobody looks behind the curtain.

Detox your culture: actions

Values are a crucial component of vibrant workplace cultures and potential employees are increasingly looking to them to determine whether it's a company that they wish to join, or not. If they're uninspiring or have remained the same despite the evolution of the business, then this could be a sign that the organization no longer takes them – or worse, their culture – seriously anymore.

But values can't be copied, created by a leadership team in a vacuum or 'rolled out' in the hope that everyone will simply adopt them. Values inform the way that work gets done, so their creation needs to be thoughtful, inclusive and provide a foundation from which people can work together.

Five things:

1. Use a collaborative approach to define your values.
2. Ensure that managers are trained on how to live the values.
3. Don't compromise the values in times of crisis.
4. Evolve the values as the business grows and changes.
5. Performance manage those people that undermine the values.

CHAPTER SIX

Do managers get it?

'There is always room to grow and ensure we are all being/
becoming the best version of ourselves in any business,
especially when it comes to leadership, to ensure that any
notion of toxicity is eradicated.'

Kelly Clarkson[1]

'Who's responsible for culture turning toxic?' It's the question I get asked the most often; frustratingly, in many cases, there's no one simple answer because, on some level, every single person involved in that culture is responsible.

Business owners or elected representatives work with senior managers to set strategy. All employees work together to build a culture to deliver on that strategy. Customers buy products or services that enable organizations to deliver their strategy. Shareholders (or in the case of government, voters) use their voting power to display their confidence in the ongoing viability of the organization and competence of its senior managers. The media also have a role to play in reporting on the health of the organization and bringing to light any issues that may negatively or positively affect current or future performance. Although let's be honest here, they mainly report the negative.

If just one link in this chain is broken, then the consequence can be catastrophic with relationships breaking down between the various groups, giving rise to behaviours or circumstances in which the culture can be considered to be toxic.

Let's take a sports team as an example. My team – Everton – is a football team from Liverpool, playing in the English Premier League. At the time of writing this in August 2023 (and I really hope things have changed by the time this book is published!), the club is mired in crisis. It's a club with a proud history, moderate – but not great – success, strong commitment to community outreach and one that was always at the forefront of innovation in the game of football.

In 2016, the club was bought by a new owner, Farhad Moshiri,[2] who promised to re-energize and 'become part of the club'.[3] He promised to inject significant amounts of money into squad development, build a new stadium and thus, on the face of it, construct the foundations for a strong future.

Fast forward seven years and over half a billion pounds has been invested in playing and coaching staff, as well as significant progress made on building a new stadium, training facilities and developing younger players. And yet, as I write, Everton are significantly worse off – in terms of league position and foundational strength – than they have ever been and the culture at the top of the organization has been described as 'toxic and dysfunctional'.[4] Even one of its own board members – the people appointed to ensure that the club is on a strong footing – said that the club 'is in turmoil'.[5]

The owner himself penned an open letter to the fans at the end of the 2021/22 season – when the club narrowly avoided relegation – stating, 'The stadium alone will not help us achieve our objectives and we are committed to not making the same mistakes again – including how we have not always spent significant amounts of money wisely.' And yet, things have regressed even further since then and the culture is rotten to the core.

January 2023 saw supporter demonstrations[6] against the strategy of the club; there were unsubstantiated allegations of threats and assault of a board member,[7] there was a vote of no-confidence from shareholders[8] and to compound all of that, the owner chose to speak to the media (rather than speaking to the fans or shareholders) to absolve himself of blame for the toxicity within the club.[9] Things were so bad that even those *reporting* on the club were being abused on social media for projecting either incorrect headlines (that supposedly sided with the club), or for not asking the right questions.

To add insult to injury, in November 2023, the club were deducted 10 points by the English Premier League for financial irregularities at a time when the owner had a deal in place to sell the club (later reduced to 6 points on appeal). The potential new owners then saw a further charge of financial mismanagement levelled at them by the Premier League in January 2024.

It would be easy to finger-point at the Premier League itself and the rules that it has in place and how fairly they are applied to each member club. However, when I look at Everton, there is no real governance, a structure that no one can understand, poor results as a result of a lack of squad depth and poor individual performance leading to disquiet on the terraces, podcasts, blogs (including me!), as well as in the pubs, in and around the city. The club is stuck in a toxic tornado. Everybody is blaming each other when the reality is that everyone is to blame in some small way. However, the buck for toxic culture *will always* stop with the leadership of an organization.

Hopefully this will all change over the coming months and years, but when it comes to building a vibrant culture, hope is not a strategy that can ever be depended upon.

The culture rots from the top

The people at the very top of a company have an ongoing opportunity to change anything that's not deemed to be working. If they wish to see their organization thrive, then it's incumbent on them to do so. Should they refuse to do so, then their leadership (and I'm using the word very loosely here) is considered to be toxic. After all, they could make the decisions to change the culture, including terminating their own tenure, yet if they refuse to do so – at times when the culture is in the media every day – this serves only to increase the toxicity. For an organization to detox its culture, then leadership from those who make decisions is absolutely essential.

As I mentioned earlier, if you're a senior manager within your organization or hold a position of influence then you may be the very reason for the toxic environment. If you're having to excuse your behaviour or that of others below you then you are complicit in those conditions being created for others. This is something that the founder of ride sharing service Uber, Travis Kalanick, realized when it was too late to do anything about the fact that he'd been sacked from his own company.

In early 2017, Uber was trapped in its own toxic tornado. A former employee wrote an article[10] about the harassment she (and others) had faced, that HR and senior management refused to act on. A report in the *New York Times*[11] highlighted technology that Uber was working on that was designed to deceive law enforcement. A competitor sued the company for corporate theft and if all that wasn't enough, Kalanick was recorded berating an Uber driver, Fawzi Kamel, in a video[12] that went viral. In the same video he also boasted to the other people in the car about the fact that he deliberately creates a 'hard' working environment.

By June and in response to investor revolt, Kalanick resigned.[13] At that time, he was also dealing with the death of his mother in an accident which also saw his father seriously injured.[14] During his leave of absence to care for his father, Kalanick penned a 2,000-word note to himself (which was published by Gizmodo in September 2019)[15] about the crisis and what he would do differently. It's a fascinating insight into his way of thinking and working, and contains some degree of regret for the toxic culture that he himself created. One set of comments particularly stood out for me.

Kalanick said, 'I put growing our business ahead of properly scaling our internal culture and organization.' 'I favoured logic over empathy, when sometimes it's more important to show you care than to prove you're right,' and finally, 'I focused on getting the right individuals to build Uber, without doing enough to ensure we're building the right kind of teams.'

This kind of thinking and behaviour is not unique to Uber; it may be prevalent in your organization right now and the people who can fix it and become catalysts for change are those at the top. Detoxing your culture requires every leader and manager within an organization (and I do mean *everyone*, from the board to the CEO to the managers who run day-to-day operations) to be committed to demonstrating the behaviours from which others can take inspiration and thus do likewise. And to ensure that there is accountability to maintain a consistency of approach.

The term 'toxic leadership' was first coined by American political scientist and author Marcia Lynn Whicker in 1996, in her book, *Toxic Leaders: When Organizations Go Bad*. She defined three styles of toxic leadership, as follows:

1. The enforcer – these people need hierarchy, certainty and money and ape the toxic styles of those that they support.
2. The street fighter – these people are egotistical, often charismatic and operate on gut-level instincts. They coordinate through rewards and punishments and like to win at all costs.
3. The bully – these people are angry, pugnacious, mad at the world and jealous of those that outperform them. They are bitter about past failures and seek to denigrate others.

Researcher Jean Lipman-Blumen describes toxic leaders as 'those individuals who, by virtue of their destructive behaviours and their dysfunctional personal qualities or characteristics, inflict serious and enduring harm on the individuals, groups, organizations, communities and even the nations that they lead'.

Employees have different words for these people, most of which are unprintable here. Words which they feel are justified by the levels of stress, hurt and anger that have been wrought upon them, sometimes over a period of years. Yet often, despite the conversation and gossip, toxic leaders are hard to spot or else do just enough to convince those above them that they have a level of competence that would be hard to replace and the toxic behaviour continues. This sounds quite calculated, because it is. Toxic leaders don't care much for anything other than their own reputation, remuneration or self-preservation. This selfishness serves no one but them and the culture suffers irrevocably as a result.

Only the leaders of an organization or team have the insights, tools, authority and influence to transform a toxic culture. Yes, they can look to others to provide a level of challenge and drive to do things differently. However, if they are not role modelling the behaviours that they expect of others then it will invariably fail. Indeed, in their research McKinsey found that over half of organizational efforts to transform culture failed as a result of leaders not wishing to change their own behaviours or else defending the status quo.

I've spoken to many employees in toxic cultures who have been gaslighted by senior managers, including those in HR, who should know better. They'll hear things such as 'that's who they are, you'll get used to them'; 'that's your perception, that's not what they mean'; 'it's meant to motivate you, not offend you'; 'you need to toughen up' and so on. Lives have been ruined by senior leaders who refused to take allegations of toxic leadership seriously. Until recently, these allegations remained tightly held in the 'black box' that was culture. Now, however, that black box is more often made of clear Perspex and available for all to see.

And in June 2021, it was Sony Music Australia who were front-page news as a result of their culture. There had been press rumblings about the culture of the organization 'since at least the mid-1990s'. These were intensified when one of their senior managers was dismissed in April of that year for the bullying and harassment of multiple staff members.

The *Guardian* newspaper conducted an investigation into the culture[16] – and its CEO Denis Handlin – which they reported on in June 2021. The investigation found that the company was 'ruled by fear'; had a culture where 'staff were expected to drink'; that even forced some members of staff to conceal pregnancies; and where abusive language and intimidating behaviour were commonplace. Only on the day the allegations were published did Sony Music release a statement saying, 'Denis Handlin will be leaving Sony Music Entertainment after more than 50 years with the company, effective immediately. It's time for a change in leadership.' They did not acknowledge the allegations made and commissioned an external review into the culture. Four more managers were released in August of that year, again with no indication of wrongdoing.[17]

Almost at the same time, allegations of toxic behaviour arose at a second music organization in Australia, Universal Music. The *Sydney Morning Herald* reported that George Ash, its president, had made inappropriate comments on a Zoom call. Ash's response was quite different to that from Sony. He sent an email to all staff saying, 'As the leader of this company I take full responsibility for creating a respectful workplace culture for everyone,' and that, 'With respect to my own behaviour, it is particularly painful to realize now that what I intended as jokes were unacceptable comments that made some of you uncomfortable.'

Ash commissioned a review into his own behaviour and conduct, subsequently addressing the feedback and retiring, reputation intact, in January 2023.

Not so for Handlin, who to date, has had many awards rescinded, including one recognizing his contribution to Australian music.[18] Sony never did publish, nor publicly acknowledge, the toxic culture allegations. However, its Australian website states: 'At Sony Music, we are all about Music and People First', not the other way around. Which maybe indicates that they haven't really learned anything from the review that they conducted.

Management isn't a popularity contest

It's really not. I understand that as a former manager myself, but you do have to work really hard to generate respect, which is generally built on the kind of human being that you are. When employees can see managers trying to do the right thing and going about it in the right way, they will respond accordingly.

One survey found, however, that almost a third of staff actively dislike their manager, with 65 per cent saying that they lacked the 'soft' skills required to build relationships with employees and get the best from them.[19] 'Soft' skills is a term still being bandied about by organizations who don't understand the importance of emotional intelligence in the workplace.

Behaviours such as empathy, compassion and active listening are crucial in creating a safe space to work. When these skills are complemented by behaviours such as discipline, presence and collaboration, managers are able to build teams where humans can thrive and goals can be achieved but the biggest challenge that managers face is a commitment to behaviour change. Many still believe that the behaviours that got them to where they are today are still relevant tomorrow. This may or may not be true depending on the behaviours being demonstrated. However, if you have a toxic culture then it is most definitely *not* true.

Toxic managers can lurk in the shadows. Often their behaviour isn't so overt as some of the case studies that I present in this book. For some, it's deliberate. They chip away at people psychologically, destroying their self-esteem and confidence. They show no concern for the welfare of others, violating their personal time, personal lives and personal sense of worth. They take all of the credit and none of the blame. They spin stories and situations to their advantage. They favour people who do what they ask without question and focus their own time on the things that they enjoy most. And yet, if results are being achieved then organizations tend to look the other way and dismiss any notion of potential wrongdoing.

I've seen it many times in organizations. Once I was approached to work with a client who had a particularly poor engagement score (<30 per cent). As part of my due diligence, I asked to see their recent engagement survey, through which I discovered that the reason for the score was one particular member of the senior management team. This person wasn't overtly badly behaved in front of their colleagues. They never swore or humiliated anyone in public; however, they had a temper, sent passive-aggressive emails, made suggestive, sometimes sexist, comments and were technically poor in areas in which they were supposed to lead. Often they talked about exceeding targets and – just in case you were missing one further sign – continually expected staff to do more with less.

When I quizzed the HR director on this, they said, 'The results speak for themselves and we would like you to help the team to toughen up so that we can continually hit those targets without excuse.' Needless to say, I declined the offer. The toxicity of a culture is a direct reflection on the leadership of an organization, so in order to detox the culture, then the entire leadership and management team – at all levels of an organization – needs to be committed to behaving differently.

In my experience, people who are continually toxic in their behaviour rarely, if ever, change and they should be removed from their positions with immediate effect. No excuses, no bureaucracy, no payouts, no apologies. These people should of course be treated with empathy and respect at the start of the process, as in, 'How can we support and help you to change your behaviour?' If no change is forthcoming, having provided this support – remaining strong and firm and not getting dragged down to their level – then there is only one action remaining to safeguard the culture for everyone else and that's dismissal.

Earlier in the book I talked about the fact that this is a situation being faced by Sir Mark Rowley, Chief Superintendent of the Metropolitan Police Force in London. Appointed to the role to address the findings of the Casey Review, he's finding that his hands are *still* tied when it comes to dealing with serial offenders.

Having expressed his frustration at not being able to remove those that shouldn't be in the force, in an interview in July 2023, he provided an update on the situation in September 2023. After almost a year in the job he said that he is 'still convinced' that hundreds of people not fit for the role that they're in, continue to be employed by the Met.[20]

Vibrant cultures don't tolerate the behaviours of toxic leaders or employees, ever.

Results matter

But what of the results? I hear you ask. How do you create a vibrant culture of success and hit targets without giving the team a volley or two? It's not actually as hard as you think, unless of course your behaviour is appalling, in which case you're on the wrong side of a heap of hard work. And possibly some coaching, counselling or a new career. Having a great culture and achieving results are inextricably linked. And generally, if you take the time, money and effort to build the former, then the latter will take care of itself.

Most leaders are impatient though and will talk a good game when it comes to culture. PwC found in one survey[21] that when they asked the question, 'Our leadership team walks the talk on purpose, values and culture?', 73 per cent of leaders agreed, but only 46 per cent of those below them did. This disparity is not unusual.

Many people are great at talking about teamwork, high performance, safety and so on, but it's only when the pressure is on to achieve results that we find out whether they mean it or not. I had one boss who told me that culture was the most important thing and then in a meeting about three weeks later (when a supplier quote came in at $9m more than we were expecting), he screamed for about three seconds, then picked up a stapler and threw it across the meeting room, shattering it on a window. In the words of that well-known anthropologist Dr Evil, 'Riiiiiiight....'

Sports teams still suffer from this 'Scream to Win' approach. There have been allegations of this behaviour in the Malaysian Olympic Swimming Team,[22] Rowing Canada,[23] the British[24] and Canadian[25] Gymnastics Teams, the Maryland Terrapins College Football Team[26] and the US National Women's Soccer League, to name a few. As Dr Gretchen Kerr, Dean and Professor of Athlete Maltreatment at the University of Toronto noted about the latter, 'Abuse in sport is never just about the perpetrator – it's about the system. It's about a system that prioritizes performance or winning over other things.'

But of course, what's the point in having a good culture if it doesn't actually achieve results? And while it's tempting to believe that taking the time to build a great culture will be the 'be-all and end-all', this is only true if that culture has something to work towards that feels just a little bit uncomfortable. Something that feels just out of reach, but in reach all at the same time. This is the irony of excellence. To be high-performing, you have to set the bar to a level that you don't immediately believe you can jump over, but that in time you come to realize is possible after all. Former basketball player Michael Jordan said it best when he said, 'You have to expect things of yourself before you can do them.' To that end and to ensure that results are achieved without the culture turning toxic, high-performing teams do the following:

Set achievable team goals – any target is best achieved when the team feels that they have a say in it, yet many goals are still set at an individual level. Of course, if you're participating in an individual endeavour, it's only right that you target personal success. However, if you're part of a team then there has to be a team element too.

The business world seems to love setting goals at a personal level too, through key performance indicators (KPIs). Then they wonder why people don't always contribute to the team. Objective Key Results (OKRs) are a much more effective way for leaders and their teams to agree on what needs to be done and by involving people in the definition of those team targets, leaders can create a different level of engagement.

Build a winning mentality – for some reason winning has become a bad thing, at least in some circles. Winning is something that cultures such as Netflix value, even going so far as to include it in their 'Culture Deck' (which is a description of how they get work done). In it, they said, 'We're a team, not a family. We're like a pro sports team, not a kid's recreational team.'[27] I like this distinction. It's important that we teach children the value of participation and being a good teammate. However, as they get older, and especially by the time they're employed, they also need to understand the value of winning. Not winning at all costs, mind. That would undermine what it means to be a good teammate. But the value and feeling of hitting targets and being part of something that takes great pride in doing so.

Learn how to disagree agreeably – sticking with the sports examples, possibly the greatest manager in football right now is Pep Guardiola. He's talked in the past about how he likes to shout at his players, but that it's built on strong relationships (see next chapter). During one televised match, one of his players – Kevin De Bruyne – shouted back at him. When asked about it after the game, Guardiola said, 'We shout at each other and I like it. Sometimes it's a little bit flat, I like this energy. It's not the first time. You don't see but he shouts at me in training. This is what we need. After that he becomes the best.'[28]

This is the thing about stretch targets: sometimes we need a gentle reminder from someone on the sidelines who can see our potential and what can be achieved. We don't have to agree in the moment – in fact, the friction that's generated through disagreeing agreeably will mean that we can fall out without the relationship suffering irrevocably.

Make quick decisions to maintain momentum – what winning teams have is the ability to make quick decisions based on the information in front of them at that point in time. According to research by decision-making experts Vroom and Jago,[29] the most successful teams make prompt decisions to maintain momentum. In their seminal work around decisions in 1973, they found that there were three elements to this: 1) Decision quality: ensure that the action is thought through; 2) Team commitment: use collaboration with team members to build trust and consensus; and 3) Time constraints: use the time that you have to guide your actions.

Winning teams recognize that it's impossible to know with 100 per cent accuracy how the decision will pan out, but without a decision, the culture – and therefore the ability to hit the target – will suffer.

Find learning in failure – aligned to the previous point is the knowledge that not everything can go to plan, some stuff is going to fail. The wrong approach to take here is to start flinging blame left, right and centre or looking for a patsy to take the fall. Well-meaning people managers may say things like, 'what doesn't kill you will make you stronger', but that's not always true and it definitely can't be assumed that people will think this way. Often they will doubt themselves and overthink their actions.

Winning teams recognize that target achievement will sometimes involve missteps and help each other to find the learning in these such that the mistakes aren't repeated and the goals compromised.

What should managers commit to?

So, in order to detox the culture, what should managers commit to doing differently? The temptation here is to write an exhaustive list of behaviours and skills. However, that may make leadership feel like *Mission: Impossible* and unlike Tom Cruise, you might not get paid millions to do this so I'm going to focus on just five things for you to think about. These five things are applicable to managers of people (executives, team leaders, coaches etc.) at all levels of an organization.

They focus on the things that instil vibrancy into the culture and provide the foundation on which to build complementary skills and behaviours.

As US–German politician Carl W. Buehner once said,[30] 'People will forget what you say, but they will never forget how you made them feel.' The goal is to become someone who has a positive impact on the lives of the human beings that they come into contact with, such that they feel good about the work that needs to get done and about themselves for doing it. These 'Culture First' managers put the team before themselves and work hard to create an environment where people feel safe to contribute and challenge while achieving the targets they've been set. 'Culture First' managers generate excitement around what's possible, which in turn instils a growth mindset.

1. *They are behavioural role models*

    It's simply not possible to build a vibrant culture free of toxicity without agreeing how people managers should behave. It can't be assumed that they automatically know what's respectful and ethical. And simply putting it into a policy won't do it either.

    Culture First managers agree how they treat others in the pursuit of goals and then role model these positive behaviours every day. They recognize that by walking the talk, they are demonstrating their personal commitment to upholding vibrant culture and showing others how it should be done. Regardless of whether it's courage, discipline, empathy, vulnerability, creativity or compassion, they understand the importance of being a good human and treating others well.

2. *They communicate clearly*

    So much management communication seems to be wrapped in a web of acronyms, pomposity or, well, long waffly sentences that don't mean an awful lot. To anyone. Clarity of messages requires simplicity – make the message easy to understand – and brevity – only use the amount of words necessary to deliver the message.

Culture First managers don't try to impress people with their level of knowledge, write the world's longest email or deliver tortuous monologues. They keep messages short, sweet and to the point, so that people feel motivated to take action, not drained of positivity, full of murderous intent.

3. *They don't tolerate toxicity*

When they spot toxic behaviour or performance, Culture First managers deal with it swiftly: they challenge it immediately and don't apologize for having to do so. They recognize that a team is only as strong as its weakest link and that it's their job to either strengthen this link or remove it and replace it with another one altogether. They understand how to have courageous conversations, and how to coach and support others to change their behaviour. They uphold the adage that no single person is more important than the team, especially if their behaviour is toxic.

4. *They walk, talk and listen*

When it comes to communication, Culture First managers ensure that they are visible and approachable at all times. They are good at setting expectations then actively make time to check in with staff to ensure that they are OK, able to progress the tasks that they have been given and – where required – offer to get their hands dirty to lighten the load on those who may be struggling.

They recognize the importance of relationships and dedicate time to maintaining them. They are present in conversations and meetings and don't allow trivialities to detract from the goals ahead of them.

5. *They develop themselves*

When Culture First leaders don't have all the answers, they go and find them or else they empower and elevate others to demonstrate their expertise. They don't sit around and moan about the things that they don't know or the organization's lack of budget available to enhance their knowledge. Instead, they actively invest money and time into their own development. They read books and blogs, listen to podcasts and undertake virtual programs to get incrementally better at what they do. They're in tune with world events to ensure that they're continually relevant in the world of work and able to get the best from everyone that reports to them.

6.   *They cooperatively build cultures*
And finally, they recognize that high performance and target achievement doesn't happen by chance. They understand that it's built on strong foundations, where employees understand each other's differences, know how to leverage them and that communication is the glue for effective collaboration.

They'll start every year with an agreement on culture and how they'll actively address the 'dumb things' that get in the way of productive work. They make time for creativity and to integrate new people into the team, and ask them to make suggestions for improvement. They bring energy, commitment and humour without expecting anything other than performance in return.

Managers aren't provided with this level of training. There's still a widespread assumption that when an individual reaches a particular level in a hierarchy or has a number of years' experience, then they immediately understand how to build a great culture. Nothing could be further from the truth.

A culture of sexual harassment, bullying and misogyny was exposed at Welsh political party Plaid Cymru in 2022. In an independent review undertaken by Nerys Evans, she found – among other things – that not only were there a lack of basic HR practices (sound familiar?) but also that managers AND politicians needed to be trained on what culture is.

The allegations led to the resignation of the Plaid Cymru leader, Adam Price. It is to be hoped, as with all case studies in this book, that the new leader, Rhun ap Iorwerth, can make education of leaders a priority to ensure this behaviour never reoccurs.

Detox your culture: actions

It's important to remember that most managers don't have 'Culture First' skills or even think about what it takes to build a vibrant culture, because it's never been part of their workplace education. Every time I run a two-day program on these skills, the feedback from experienced managers is almost always 'I wish I'd have had this knowledge 10 years ago!'

It's little wonder that cultures turn toxic when people are promoted but aren't provided with the skills required to create vibrant cultures or the behaviours expected of them aren't continually reinforced. And let's be honest, some people – the ones without the people skills – should never be promoted in the first place.

Given that management behaviour and skillset is continually cited as the reason why people leave their organization, it's not something that can be left to chance.

Five things:

1. Provide managers with the skills to build teams and reduce the risk of toxic culture.
2. Get the team involved in goal setting.
3. Ensure that communications are clear and free from confusion.
4. Don't tolerate poor behaviours from any manager at any level.
5. Ensure that managers are role models for all employees.

CHAPTER SEVEN

Does empathy exist?

'Being treated like a human being was sadly not always a
given for those working at BrewDog.'

Punks With Purpose Open Staff Letter to BrewDog Owners[1]

When employees feel connected to each other and to the company
that they work for they are likely to be four times more productive
than if they're not.[2] And for teams to achieve goals, productivity is very
important. When people feel disconnected from each other and from
the company then not only do results suffer, but it also affects how they
feel about themselves, about others and the chances of a toxic culture
increase.

Feeling 'emotionally connected' is something that as humans we're
continually on the lookout for, not just in work but in our personal
lives too. Indeed, Emotionally Focused Therapy (EFT)[3] is frequently
used by professionals to help individuals, couples and families. It's
used to understand how emotions drive thoughts and actions. From
that, they help people to establish the 'map' of how to build and evolve
strong relationships with others.

EFT centres on *attachment theory*, which neuroscientists believe is a
key requirement for all humans. They believe that there are 'networks
of neurons' in the brain committed to helping us to not only create
emotional bonds, but also being just fine when we're left on our own
too. This starts when we're born, developing between infant and
caregiver,[4] and continues into our adult lives too.[5]

Creating these human-to-human bonds is called different things in different cultures. Here are some examples:

Māori (New Zealand) – 'Whakawhanaungatanga': This term represents the process of building relationships, connecting with others and establishing a sense of belonging. It's an important concept in Maori culture that promotes inclusivity and mutual respect.

Japanese – 'Kizuna': This term refers to the strong emotional bonds and connections between individuals. It emphasizes the importance of deepening relationships and fostering a sense of unity and support within a community.

Hawaiian – 'Aloha Spirit': Aloha Spirit is a concept in Hawaiian culture that represents the attitude of love, compassion and kindness towards others. It embodies the idea of forming connections and treating people with respect and understanding.

South African – 'Ubuntu': Ubuntu is a Nguni Bantu term that translates to 'humanity towards others'. It emphasizes the interconnectedness of all people and encourages showing empathy, caring and solidarity in building relationships.

Navajo (Native American) – 'K'é': K'é encompasses the concept of kinship and interconnectedness in Navajo culture. It signifies the importance of maintaining strong relationships, supporting family and community, and living in harmony with others.

Indian – 'Namaste': Namaste is a traditional Indian greeting that is often accompanied by a slight bow with hands pressed together. It expresses a sense of respect and acknowledgement of the divine spark within each person, emphasizing the interconnectedness of all beings.

It's only natural, therefore, that we should want to develop human-to-human bonds with the people that we work with. People of all ages and genders find people through work that they share interests, points of view and relationships with. Indeed, I met two of my best friends through work, as well as my wife! Almost three quarters of employees share their hopes and dreams with their colleagues and 83 per cent say that developing a strong 'work family' makes them happier.[6] However, this doesn't mean that people have to be best friends (a common misconception), live in each other's pockets or occupy the same space all of the time. Indeed, being best friends can often get in the way of productive work, lead to favouritism or inappropriate/unethical behaviour. For example, one general manager that I knew employed his best friend and would repeatedly make excuses for his bad behaviour, when others who did likewise were performance managed.

That said, most organizations lack either the commitment or desire to ever get to the point where connections are even created in the first place. Insisting instead on productivity, efficiency and the pursuit of excellence without investing time and effort into building emotional connection between people. Most will simply assume that people will figure each other out and find ways to work together and in the absence of any structure, that's exactly what will happen. Unfortunately, there is a significantly increased chance that those relationships will be built on assumptions or stereotypes. 'The loud one', 'the quiet one', 'the nerd', 'the positive one', 'the angry one', 'the emotional one' and so on.

In most of the toxic cultures that I've worked with people have not found ways to connect. They avoid difficult conversations, there's no trust, they don't mix socially, they doubt that anyone is working as hard as they are and there's no commitment to improve their situation until someone else makes the first move! And it doesn't matter how big or small the organization is, when toxic relationships exist between employees then it can hit the news at any time.

Take the Toronto-based radio station Q107. Unless you live in the Greater Toronto area you're unlikely to have heard of it, right? And yet in 2022 it hit the news headlines after one of its presenters released a

13-minute video on social media accusing a co-worker (not manager) of abusive behaviour.

Jennifer Valentyne said in her video: 'What would you do if a co-worker screamed at you, belittled you, called you names, shut you out, brought you to tears and then laughed when he told you to cry all you want?' Oh, and if you think that's bad, none of her co-workers seemingly intervened. She said, 'All these [sic] while three other men watched uncomfortably, yet supported him because they knew what would happen to them if they went against him.' She reported it not only to the station, but also the Canadian Human Rights Commission, citing gender discrimination.[7]

The subject of this (and other) allegations, radio broadcaster John Derringer, was investigated and left the company after being suspended from his role.[8] Many allegations had been made about his behaviour and had never been acted on by HR.[9]

Emotional capital

Emotional capital is the 'feelings and beliefs that help employees to form successful relationships with each other'. Cultures with lots of emotional capital create a sense of belonging for the people who work in them and individuals are committed to building the relationships required for all team members to be successful. According to Paul Thagard, author and Professor Emeritus at the University of Waterloo, attachment is just one element of emotional capital.[10] In order for people to be successful (whatever it means for them) in their working and personal lives, he suggests that the following are required:

Self-esteem
Self-esteem stems from self-awareness and centres on you having a positive opinion of yourself. When you have self-esteem, you value your thoughts, experiences, skills and actions. Your self-esteem is shaped by the culture you work in, values and societal status.

Self-regulation

Self-regulation also requires self-awareness and centres on the control of undesirable behaviours, thoughts and actions in relation to your goals. When you learn how to self-regulate, you avoid potentially destructive habits or actions and can stay calm in a crisis.

Emotional energy

Emotional energy relates to the passion and enthusiasm you have for your work (or not!). The amount of energy you feel will have a direct impact on your attitudes and your mindset. Your feelings can positively or negatively affect your energy levels throughout the day.

Attachment

Attachment – as discussed – is the ability that you have to form emotional bonds with other human beings. The level to which you feel attached to those around you will drive your social, emotional and cognitive development.

Resilience

Resilience is the art of being able to bounce back from a challenge and move forward, potentially becoming better than you were before. When you are resilient, you are able to see the learning inherent in failure and adjust future actions to ensure that the mistake isn't repeated.

Agreeableness

Agreeableness is a trait that generates likeability, kindness, approachability, warmth, cooperation and tact. People who are agreeable have greater degrees of empathy (the glue that holds teams together) and find it easier to trust others.

Optimism

Optimism is a belief that everything will work out as planned or else generate positive outcomes. Optimism isn't about 'positive thinking' per se, it is about being able to sense possibility or opportunity in even the most negative situations.

Of course, it's simply impossible for everyone in a team to do all of these things, all of the time, at the same time! Without making the time to understand oneself and others around you, the chances of it occurring reduce to almost zero and accelerate the chances of a toxic tornado. The way to avoid this is to dramatically increase the amount of empathy that exists between team members.

Getting to know yourself and each other

Empathy is defined as the ability to understand or feel what another person is experiencing. 'In organizational awareness,' writes Chade-Meng Tan in his book, *Search Inside Yourself*, 'you understand the feelings, needs and concerns of individual people and how those interact with those of others and the organization as a whole.'

What he's saying is that in cultures of self-aware individuals, you 'get' each other and adjust the way you interact with each other as a consequence. In this environment, relationships are easy to build – as people are open to doing so – and agreements formed on how work will get done. This in turn creates a 'safe' environment within which work can get done and as a result, emotional capital is enhanced (see the next chapter for more on this).

What's required to get to this point is deeper understanding. People need to understand themselves better and what it takes to contribute to true team success. In doing so, ipso facto, a work culture also evolves and the chances for toxicity diminish. Too many organizations are still trying to change culture with technology, some with the latest method of choice. The first place to start is yourself.

By focusing on the capacity to be self-aware, you'll begin to understand the things that your personality is naturally good at, as well as those that you need to work on, and how to utilize feedback to continue to grow as a person. In addition, greater self-awareness allows you to provide others with feedback and advice on their behaviours too, so that the team can co-create a safe environment where everyone understands each other and can function together effectively.

The problem is, many people aren't very self-aware. According to author Tasha Eurick, 95 per cent of people think that they're self-aware and yet in reality, only about 15 per cent are.[11] And at times, I feel like there's more chance of AI becoming self-aware before people in toxic cultures do! People who lack self-awareness aren't open to feedback and can't regulate their emotional responses. Consequently, workplace cultures have difficulty evolving positively in order to achieve results.

In my experience of working with global organizations to help them change their cultures, I see this issue – lack of individual self-awareness – all the time. But, I also see that when it's addressed head-on, it makes a huge difference. Not only to the happiness of staff, enhanced emotional capital and increased cultural belonging, but also to team results. That is to say, the bottom line.

In 2013, researchers Zes and Landis in their paper, 'A Better Return on Self Awareness',[12] found that, 'Poor-performing companies' employees were 79 per cent more likely to have low overall self-awareness than those at firms with robust ROR (return on results)'. They also found that companies with a greater percentage of self-aware employees consistently outperformed those with a lower percentage.

In order to consistently avoid toxic cultures AND deliver results, there must be an acceptance, particularly from managers and team leaders, that not everyone is as self-aware as they need to be in order to contribute to team success. Personalities vary, that's true. But cultural acceptance of people who lack self-awareness – which in turn gives rise to toxic behaviour – is not a good thing. As you'd imagine there is lots of research in this area, but essentially, there are two elements of self-awareness:

1. External – I'm starting with this one first because the workplaces with the most vibrant cultures do it really well: feedback from others.

Key to changing your behaviour, or at least better understanding how you're perceived in a working context, is to actively seek feedback from people whose goal is to help you become a better human. Not people who are looking to throw stones at you, but those who want to help you help yourself. Gaining these regular insights will provide a pathway for continual emotional maturity. In my experience, this feedback works best when it's sought from different people, in different roles from different generations. If you merely seek it from the people around you, they are more likely to tell you what you want to hear or make excuses for the behaviours that you demonstrate. External self-awareness will challenge the unconscious opinions that you have of the way that you present yourself.

2. Internal – this centres around what you know about yourself: your personality, values, passions, experiences, interests and goals. You're at your most self-aware when your internal voice is guiding your thoughts and actions or else when you replay a situation and 'talk to yourself' about what you'd learned and what you'd repeat or do differently next time. Regret – while painful – can actually aid the process of self-awareness as it can help you to make decisions on the habits you need to change. However, being *too* self-aware can also undermine your confidence and lead to self-doubt and criticism. The trick is to find a balance between understanding the set of skills you were born with, having a plan to develop the things that you lack and to use this knowledge to inform how you'll interact with others.

Interestingly, when people in toxic cultures are called out for their behaviour, often you will hear them say, 'I'm going to take some time to reflect on my actions.' Which is just what P.J. Vogt, host of the 'Reply All' podcast, did in 2021 after complaints from colleagues about his contribution to a toxic culture – centred on unionization of staff at Gimlet Media.

Vogt released a statement on Twitter, saying that he was taking time away from the show 'to think and to listen'.[13] While this is a noble and not insignificant thing to do, being introspective doesn't always improve how self-aware you are. In fact, research from 2019 found that those who introspect are actually *less* self-aware![14] Of course, people can't tell you to be self-aware and it immediately change everything. You have to take on feedback and educate yourself about, well, yourself. Personality profiles can be very helpful in this process.

Almost all personality surveys in the marketplace today[15] (in the US, it's estimated that organizations spend over $500m a year) are based on psychology pioneer Carl Jung's human personality and behaviour work from the 1920s. He posited that personality traits are stable characteristics of individual differences that may be used to describe and explain behaviour. That is, we do certain things consistently and without thinking.

Jung found that these common traits are reliant on three things:

- How people gather information (sensing or intuition)
- How people make decisions (thinking or feeling)
- How people react in social situations (introversion or extroversion).

Broadly, when you put this information together, our personalities are made up of varying percentages of four different elements, which I've renamed to make them more applicable to the language we use in workplace cultures today: detail, people, action and social.

No one is a 'pure' version of just one of these four elements, that's not how it works. And no one can put any human in a box and declare: that's you! We are complex beings. Most of us have a percentage of each element as part of our personality, but it's the predominant preference that generally guides how we see the world, make decisions and act in social situations.

I've long advocated the use of personality profiles – not for their often-definitive 'this is who you are!' reports, more to generate interest in self-awareness and how it can benefit both the individual and the team. When you have this more detailed understanding of your personality and are able to keep it front of mind, you are able to recognize and moderate your emotions accordingly, noticing almost immediately when you've acted or behaved in a way that runs counter to what you consider to be your 'normal' way of reacting. Crucially, your capacity for empathy also increases.

Eighty-five per cent of managers in one *Harvard Business Review* publication[16] said that empathy is a more important skill now than it was before the pandemic; Gartner[17] found that managers that display empathy have as much as three times the impact on employee performance, while Mercer's Global Talent Trends report[18] recognized 'empathetic management' as the third most important skill (after a growth mindset and collaboration).

A survey of over 5,000 workers conducted by Paper Giant[19] found that almost half of those surveyed now had an increased need for empathy. This demonstrates that there has been a definitive shift from technical to emotional leadership, particularly in the eyes of the next generation of employees.

One study from Business Solver at the end of 2020[20] found that 83 per cent of Gen Z employees would 'choose an employer with a strong culture of empathy over an employer offering a slightly higher salary'. Millennials and Gen Z employees are simply not going to put up with the working environments that Baby Boomer and Gen X employees tolerated. They are prioritizing fairness and flatly refuse to accede to cultural practices they consider to be toxic. Indeed, they are mobilizing like never before. In 2021, 20-year-old Laila Dalton alleged that she was subjected to maltreatment at the hands of her managers at a Starbucks in Arizona, USA. She recorded the interactions on her phone and the video subsequently went viral. (Note: In Arizona, permission to record conversations where the person recording is present is not required.)[21]

Prior to the recording, Dalton and three of her co-workers had been looking to form a union at the store in order to protect the rights and mental health of workers there. She was handed a reprimand when handing out union cards to members. The level of harassment increased, so Dalton started recording all of her conversations as a way of protecting her rights, an action that the National Labor Relations Board said had[22] ultimately led to her dismissal.

Starbucks drafted founder Howard Schultz back in to be interim CEO and he declared war on unionization, saying at a town hall meeting that the company was 'being assaulted in many ways by [their] threat'. Staff and unions hit back in 2022, staging a walkout at one store as a result of alleged employee maltreatment that catapulted the coffee giant into the news. Later that year, in June in an interview with the *New York Times*, Schultz talked about the generational shift in expectations, saying, 'Gen Z has a different view of the world.' He continued, 'I'm an old-school person and this is a different generation.'

An Arizona judge ultimately found that Starbucks had not fired Dalton for unionizing.[23]

Generating generational empathy

According to the OC Tanner Global Culture Report,[24] culture is the number-one requirement of every generation; however, Gen Z employees rated it the highest, over 10 per cent higher than Gen X. These generational expectations represent a big challenge to organizations looking to create a great employee experience, minimize the risk of toxicity and create a culture that inspires emotional capital, productive work and loyalty in all, regardless of age. Seventy-five per cent of managers in one OC Tanner survey[25] believe that it's their biggest challenge. And each generation thinks that the one before them is the problem and doesn't understand any after them! Honestly, kids today...

For clarity, the generations are broadly considered to be 15 years in length and segmented (by birth year) as follows:

Baby Boomers: 1946–64

Gen X: 1965–80

Millennials: 1981–96

Gen Z: 1997–2010

Gen A: 2011 –

Of course, putting people into boxes is something that authors like to do in order to justify a narrative. However (and in my defence), it's true to say that every generation is united by similar challenges and opportunities, values and ideologies, particularly in relation to where they live and work. These 'clues' provide insights into why people may think and act a particular way.

Clues may centre on the impact of technology, changing attitudes towards gender and identity, global events and movements and language. All of these elements can have a significant impact on the upbringing of humans and generate different ways of thinking, feeling and acting. And of course, that means that they will have a significant impact on the world of work. For example, my parents' generation never used technology in the workplace (with the exception of early word processors) and continually struggle to understand why people would not only keep a computer in their pocket, but also let it drain their attention. In comparison, my children's generation (Gen Z) can't understand why you wouldn't have a device to hand at all times. Just in case they might want to look up how many emails are sent (globally) every day! It's about 300bn when I last counted...

Of course, it's not just technology. How we behave towards each other as humans has changed. When I started work in the mid-1980s my dad told me to keep my head down, not cause trouble and do as the boss says regardless of whether they were right or not. In those days, hearing managers berate staff publicly was commonplace, women were routinely disrespected, harassed and worse, while winning at all costs was expected in achieving results.

In Australia in 2022, building materials company James Hardie fired its CEO, Jack Truong.[26] He was dismissed from his job for 'intimidating, threatening and disrespectful behaviour towards colleagues'. Almost immediately, Truong fired back, saying that he was 'blindsided by the termination and unequivocally reject the assertions made by the company' and that he delivered 'substantial sales and profit growth while its share price more than tripled'.[27]

The company, through a spokesperson, was forced to reiterate that the board had provided 'clear feedback and counselling on the impact that Mr Truong's behaviours were having on his colleagues on multiple occasions' and the sacking stood.[28]

There are so many issues at play here: expectation setting, self-awareness, behaviour and an understanding of how the world has changed. Achievement at the emotional expense of staff is simply not acceptable in today's working world. The 'it wasn't like that in my day' attitude routinely overlooks just how inhumane workplaces were (and unfortunately for some, still are). Workplace nostalgia is only ever useful if it's used as fuel for learning, not as an anchor to hold back progress.

Like I said, while it's far too simplistic to put people in boxes, in toxic multi-generational workplaces you'll almost certainly hear things such as 'that's typical Boomer behaviour', 'these Millennials have it easy', 'the problem with this generation is…', and so on. Empathy is required to not only understand the personalities of others, but also in helping to educate each other on how they see their world today, wherever they may be.

Communicating successfully

As a result of better understanding yourself and others, you will be better able to respond to them in a way that they appreciate. This is the 'treat people in a way you like to be treated yourself' lesson that your parents, guardians or teachers tried to instil into you when you were young! A key element of this is the ability to change the way that you communicate when speaking to others with different personalities. Without self-awareness, you will simply adopt the communication style that best befits your preferences. However, once you learn to understand the preferences of others, it means you will be able to 'step outside yourself' and communicate in a way that other people can hear and relate to.

Red Bull Racing are often seen as being cut-throat when it comes to dealing with driver underperformance, yet they recognize the importance of empathy in communicating with different personalities in different ways in order to motivate their drivers to achieve high performance. At time of writing this book, they have two drivers on their roster: Max Verstappen (very much an *action* personality) and Sergio Pérez (very much a *people* personality).

When asked by the media about Pérez's disappointing outing at the British Grand Prix in 2023, team principal Christian Horner said: 'He's the type of guy that just needs an arm around his shoulder and you work with him.' This variable communication style is a key demonstration of what it means to be self-aware.

Each of the four personalities requires a different communication approach and when employed correctly, will enhance empathy between individuals:

Detail:
- Slow-paced
- Talk in bullet points
- Require context and time to think
- Don't want to be put on the spot
- Will want facts, figures, data and logic.

People:
- Friendly approach
- Talk to them, not *at* them

- Require time to process what's being asked of them
- Don't like to be put on a pedestal
- Will want to maintain a harmonious approach.

Action:
- Direct and bold
- Want to be told what needs to be done in the shortest time possible
- Will ask questions, so be prepared!
- Don't want to be told how to do it
- Will want a deadline.

Social:
- Outgoing and enjoys humour
- Need to inspire them with energy
- Will look to be creative
- Will want to be introduced to others who can help
- Will need to be closely managed so that they stay on task!

As I mentioned earlier in this chapter, no one is a perfect match for these definitions. However, in the absence of a relationship with others who have shared their preferences with you, this list is a good starting point.

Communication breakdowns occur frequently in alleged toxic cultures and often it is simply misunderstood preferences. If I have a direct style and I choose to consistently use it on someone whose style is different from mine, then they could consider that to be inappropriate and toxic. That's not to say that I'm swearing or *being* inappropriate in my language or actions. I'm simply not thinking of their needs and choosing instead to impose my own style upon them. It can be similarly frustrating if I'm someone who likes to provide unstructured thinking, seeks too much input or requires every bit of detail before undertaking a task.

In many situations, alleged toxicity can be addressed by helping people to better understand each other, as it did with a team I worked with in New Zealand in 2023. By understanding their own communication preferences and those of the people around them, they were better able to recognize different styles and also moderate their own style when working with others. As a result, engagement and productivity both increased and camaraderie between team members was greatly improved.

Camaraderie is a great word to describe the empathy that humans have for each other. Its origins are French.[29] Prior to 1571, the word 'camarade' was used in a military context and meant 'group sleeping in one room', but by the late sixteenth century, it was used to represent 'one who shares with someone else'. It entered the English language in the nineteenth century as camaraderie and means 'mutual trust and friendship among a group of people who spend time together'.

One report[30] found that when teams develop *above average* (so, not even great!) camaraderie, they are eight times more likely to produce great work, five times more likely to generate cultural satisfaction and 11 times more likely to achieve their results. But as you will have seen throughout this chapter, camaraderie isn't something that can be forced. In fact, if it reads like hard work, then that's because it is! But then, whoever said that being a consistently good human being in the workplace was easy to do?

Detox your culture: actions

When you take time to build empathy and camaraderie you will enhance the emotional capital between employees and generate a mindset that believes – through the strength of its people – that anything is possible. Where camaraderie is weak there is blame, apathy, rigidity, individuality, communication breakdowns and a lack of trust in others to do the right thing. In other words, it's the perfect breeding ground for a toxic culture.

Skills such as empathy, vulnerability and resilience, previously described as 'soft skills', are now considered to be essential in supporting employees, maintaining trust and connection, and ultimately, delivering results to shareholders and/or the general public. These are also skills that employees expect to see from their managers – they are not a 'nice to have'. Organizations that systematically hire for emotional intelligence actively reduce the risk of toxic culture by creating bonds between employees that are hard to break.

Five things:

1. Increase self-awareness.
2. Help people to improve through regular feedback.
3. Practise different communication styles.
4. Actively build camaraderie.
5. Remind people that success is a team effort.

CHAPTER EIGHT

How does work get done?

'I did work for someone once who ran such a volatile, hostile
set that it made me physically ill. My eyes were swelling up,
I was absorbing all of this nuttiness.'

Melissa McCarthy – actor[1]

Connecting humans deliberately to the point where empathy exists
is still no guarantee that those people will work together in a way
that generates consistent high performance or produces outputs
in line with expectations. Self-aware individuals have the capacity
for collaboration; however, one further step is required to make
this a reality. And that is, a simple agreement on *how* work will
be done.

Vanessa Druskat, Psychologist at the University of New Hampshire,
surveyed high-performing teams back in 2001 and she found that
results were achieved not only through the collective high emotional
intelligence (EI) of team members, but also through agreed norms
between them. In fact, they proved that the former is actually dependent
on the latter: 'For a team to have high EI, it needs to create norms that
establish mutual trust among members, a sense of group identity, and a
sense of group efficacy. These three conditions are essential to a team's
effectiveness because they are the foundation of true cooperation and
collaboration.'[2]

So while it's important to understand each other's personalities
and communication preferences, it is also important to the delivery
of results, to understand how you'll work together to achieve them.

These 'norms' or 'principles' of collaboration take into consideration the following:

- How people will behave towards each other
- How individuals will interact to achieve common goals
- How leadership will be established
- How plans will be formed and executed
- How the group will hold each other accountable
- How often work will be reprioritized
- How technology should be used to support the work that needs to be done
- How group safety will be maintained.

While compromising any of these can lead to toxicity, by far the biggest cause is how humans choose to behave towards each other. HR have policies that are used to enforce, but these are almost always used retrospectively when what is required in order to avoid toxic culture in the first place is proactivity in agreeing what's appropriate and what's not.

It's tempting to believe that self-aware employees understand, by default, how to behave. However, this is to assume that everyone is not only in control of their emotions all of the time, but also that they have the same understanding of what it means to be a good human being (in a team context). And that's simply not true.

That's not to say that people deliberately show up to work determined to be the worst version of themselves, although it may seem this way for some! No employee – in my experience – ever gets up in the morning determined to be the worst version of themselves. They don't look at themselves in the mirror and boldly declare that they're going to be the worst kind of employee. One that gets in the way of productive work. One that openly disrespects those around them or acts selfishly when part of a team. And yet, many people have found themselves in situations where they have behaved in ways that betray who they are, including me.

In one of my early management roles, I once sent a late-night email to the entire leadership team email group – that I was part of – openly questioning the value that a consulting organization was adding to the work that we were doing, as well as the quality provided in relation to the money spent. But I didn't stop there. I also questioned the technical ability of their managing director in supporting our transformation efforts. Except, unbeknownst to me (but in no way excusing my actions), the managing director was included in the email group, leading to a very public – and utterly humiliating – apology from which I learned a lot.

My excuse at the time was that the stress of work had forced me into losing control of my emotions. Of course, it was simply that – an excuse – and yet there was an element of validity to it.

At the time we simply had too many priorities, for which we had little clarity, our boss was unapproachable (or went missing for long periods) and as a leadership team we were all focused on doing our own thing rather than working together to better understand how we felt and needed to behave in order to best serve the team.

We'd flicked the switch to angry autopilot.

In their 1988 research paper entitled, 'The Mindlessness of Organizational Behaviours', authors Blake Ashforth and Yitzhak Fried found that employees 'go on automatic' following 'established rules'. What this means is that toxic cultures can often turn good people bad, as employees copy the behaviours of those around them in order to either fit in or as an act of self-preservation.

This was an accusation levelled at the comedy show *Saturday Night Live* (*SNL*) by author and reporter Maureen Ryan. In her book, *Burn it Down: Power, Complicity, and a Call for Change in Hollywood*, she alleged that the workplace at SNL is a place where 'abuse and toxicity are not just permitted but often celebrated'.

Former *SNL* writer Steven W. Thrasher also wrote about his experiences in the *Guardian*,[3] saying the culture was one that 'pitted everyone against each other'. While a group of female employees, speaking anonymously, said that the environment was 'routinely uncomfortable, incredibly sexist, and at times unsafe'.[4]

Safe to belong and perform

This workplace 'safety' that the writers alluded to is something that organizations around the world now take seriously, and it's long overdue. Psychological safety (to give it its full name) wasn't a 'thing' when I and many other people my age started work and yet looking back, I distinctly remember when it was there and when it wasn't.

It wasn't a course that was mandated by HR or something that the CEO talked about. It was just something that myself and the other people around me did when we were able to be the best versions of ourselves and when we cared for each other and what the team and organization were trying to achieve.

When we did this, it felt 'safe' to speak up, challenge the status quo and the behaviours of others and to take time out when we just weren't on our game. We didn't take it for granted. Instead, we spent time sharing stories, generating ideas, trading skills and making the effort to get to know each other outside of work to strengthen the connections we had, such that we were able to agree to and uphold the norms we created.

I recently traded LinkedIn messages with a former colleague of 20 years ago and his words got me thinking about this topic. He said, 'I miss those days. Everything felt easy and yet it wasn't. Deadlines were tight, pressure was high, we didn't always see eye to eye and yet we loved every minute of it.' And we did, because we had each other's backs. We'd taken the time to agree how we'd behave towards each other, define what we were aiming for and how we'd ensure that the way we worked together remained productive and rewarding.

Safety is something that all the great teams, projects, departments and organizations have, yet I also remember the times when safety was lacking. There was fear, arguing, bullying, intimidation, anxiety, stress and tears. People's names and titles were used as sticks to intimidate others with. Unreasonable demands were placed on time, energy or emotions and anyone who mentioned any of these things was reminded of the importance of the work or that everyone was in the same boat and we just had to 'shut up and get it done'.

Any outburst of emotion would be dealt with using phrases such as:

'You need to toughen up'
'You can't do/say anything these days'
'Stop being so touchy'
'In the old days...'
'I didn't mean it'
'It's only a bit of fun'.

Except it wasn't. In fact, it was the very antithesis of fun. It was physically and psychologically damaging, and it ruined people's lives. That particular example occurred many years ago for me and yet little has changed for many people in teams around the world.

In 2022, the World Health Organization (WHO) published statistics[5] showing that over 260m people worldwide suffer from mental health issues as a result of their work. And that days lost as a result of mental health issues cost businesses over \$1 trillion in lost productivity every year.

Many sporting cultures are yet to take mental health seriously and continue to use old-fashioned, borderline abusive approaches to 'motivate' athletes that serve only to undermine their mental health. Of course, the mental health of athletes was simply not a priority in the 'old days' and people of all genders, ages and abilities were often labelled as weak, soft or not having the fire in the bellies to compete.

One of the most high-profile cases in recent years was that of Olympic champion gymnast, Simone Biles. As the highest-profile member of the gymnastic team at the 2020 Summer Olympics in Tokyo, Biles was widely expected to win every competition that she entered. And yet, after qualifying for all the individual finals, she took to Instagram to announce, 'I truly do feel like I have the weight of the world on my shoulders at times. I know I brush it off and make it seem like pressure doesn't affect me but damn sometimes it's hard.'[6]

It was the first sign that she was struggling. The next day, after suffering a bout of the 'twisties' (where a gymnast suddenly loses their sense of where their body is in space during an intense routine), Biles withdrew from the team event, citing mental health issues. She later said she'd been inspired by tennis player Naomi Osaka, who'd done a similar thing when withdrawing from the French Open tournament.[7]

It was an incredibly brave thing for Biles to do and she was roundly applauded for her actions. At the time she said, 'I say put mental health first. Because if you don't, then you're not going to enjoy your sport and you're not going to succeed as much as you want to', yet there were also deeper issues with the USA Gymnastic culture.[8]

Biles had suffered sexual assault at the hands of Larry Nassar in 2018, as had many other athletes and at a senate hearing into the abuse in 2021,[9] she blamed 'an entire system that enabled and perpetuated his abuse', stating that USA Gymnastics and the US Olympic and Paralympic committees had failed to do their jobs.[10]

Former teammate Aly Raisman backed up Biles' claims by saying, 'USA Gymnastics has been an absolute disaster for years and unfortunately not enough has changed for us to believe in a safer future.'

USA Gymnastics have since answered some of these concerns and taken small steps to rebuild the trust between athletes, coaches and the organization. To the point where Biles has now returned to competition. In an email to CNN in 2023, USA Gymnastics spokesperson Jill Geer welcomed her return (and that of other athletes) and said, 'That elite gymnastics is a sport they want to come back to reinforces that USA Gymnastics has been on the right track with our cultural transformation. It is something we continue to work on every day.'[11]

A coach's, and for that matter, manager's role is not only to focus on the technical aspects that require improvement, but also to assess the emotional maturity and capacity of the person in their 'care' and choose the right approach to motivate them without destroying their confidence or mental health in the process.

The same WHO survey I mentioned earlier found that 'For every US$1 put into scaled up treatment for common mental disorders, there is a return of US$4 in improved health and productivity.' This is not just about creating a gold-plated well-being program, it's about creating a workplace that never needs to use it.

Psychological safety

Amy Edmondson is the leading global authority on psychological safety, Novartis Professor of Leadership and Management at Harvard Business School and a best-selling author. She's been advocating for safety in teams since her book, *Teaming*, was released in 2012. In an interview a couple of years back, she described safety thus: 'Psychological safety fundamentally is all about candour – creating conditions whereby people can be far more candid than is normal or natural, but if we're gonna be candid, then we're gonna find some things hurtful.' She continued, 'So it's this emotional resilience, the muscle of being able to bounce back quickly when things don't go exactly the way you wanted them to, is much more important than ever.'[12]

As she describes in her book, psychological safety isn't about staying in a comfort zone, it's about building an environment where it's OK to take risks, such that you can continually learn, as an individual and as a team.

Owners, executives, managers and employees of teams, projects, departments and organizations around the world need to understand that only through the deliberate creation of a workplace where every member feels safe to contribute, speak up, challenge and do their best work can they ever hope to achieve their goals, whatever they may be.

These workplaces need to recognize the effects that the behaviours of others can have on those around them and take steps to lead with empathy, not anger, to deal with issues swiftly and positively, and restore the kind of environment that people want to be connected to, not run away from. Far too many cultures still make excuses for behaviour of employees at all levels or fail to deal with it in a timely and appropriate manner and find themselves in the media. Here are some high-profile examples:

- Gaming and esports energy drink company G Fuel terminated the employment of seven managers, a day after five of them contacted HR to report their CEO's use of offensive language.[13]
- An independent report into employee behaviour at air traffic controllers, Airservices Australia, found that one in two people had been bullied and one in five sexually assaulted. One person was quoted as saying, 'The culture [in this Tower] is totally toxic. It's like *Lord of the Flies* or *Animal Farm*.'[14]
- A report into toxic cultures at fire departments across the US found that 80 per cent of males and 87 per cent of females have 'witnessed or experienced verbal harassment from a colleague' and that 55 per cent of females 'have been or know of someone who has been inappropriately touched by a co-worker'.[15]
- An investigation into Indian educational software company, Byju, by Reuters found that staff were made to work longer hours under threats and that employees said that the success of the company 'is built on the back of an abusive and exploitative work environment and unscrupulous sales practices'.[16]

In almost all of these cases the organizations at the centre of the allegations did nothing to stop the behaviour happening in the first place, or, as is the case with Byju, plead their innocence, saying that they uphold the 'highest safe workplace standards'.

Another excuse I often hear is that unionized employees need to be treated differently as people than non-unionized employees and this is simply not true. As a former member of unions myself, I never once believed that the rules around behaviour were different for me than for those who didn't belong to a union.

There is a process to follow for all employees when working to create a safe environment and no one should be allowed to undermine it. The formal process needs to be followed and if the person refuses to change their behaviour and continues to undermine safety then they need to be exited from the business, regardless of their union membership or not. Unions for their part need to support this, not defend it, and ensure that they are seen as protecting the rights of all workers, not condoning the behaviours of one individual, that undermine the conditions for others.

Creating safety in teams matters: it generates the conditions that lead to business results. It helps human beings to fulfil their purpose, create a sense of fun and provide an environment that fosters a growth mindset, welcomes ideas and where people can continually challenge each other to be better. It also rids the workplace of those who don't wish to change, whose behaviours are rooted in selfishness or a desire to exert their influence – in every egregious way – over others. These people cannot be allowed to prevail and undermine the psychological and physical safety that all organizations need to provide for its employees.

Toxic productivity

Among all the statistics in the Gallup State of the Global Workforce report in 2022,[17] one really stood out to me and that centred on stress. Gallup found that almost half of the people interviewed said that they'd experienced a lot of stress the previous day and that only a third of people felt like their well-being was 'thriving'.

Now, of course some stress can be a good thing. It can motivate us, help us to build meaningful relationships with others and lift our confidence once we've achieved a goal that requires us to step outside of our comfort zone. But experiencing a lot of stress is beneficial to no one and is the reality for many people every single day as a result of the culture within which they work.

In 2022, the New South Wales state government in Australia made the news.[18] Here's a brief summary of the story. Lots of senior people knew that there was poor behaviour going on, chose to do absolutely nothing about it for years, then expressed their shock and disappointment when the allegations were finally made public. The then State Premier Dominic Perrottet, when interviewed, said, 'Clearly we have a culture in the NSW parliament that over time has become, in many instances, toxic and wrong.'

In this environment, often a fairly 'standard' approach is taken. Consultants are employed to write a report that takes far too long to produce; senior leaders talk up things like 'culture change', 'diversity and inclusion', 'well-being programs' and 'safe place to work' but ultimately refuse to address the real problems. Namely, the behaviours of certain individuals that they'll continue to walk past in the hope that they'll change – they won't.

An absence of courage to do something about this or to try a different approach means that the health of workers will continue to be adversely affected, through no fault of their own. The toxicity will prevail until it becomes someone else's problem to deal with, then the cycle will be repeated.

In Australia, there is a dedicated day that focuses on mental health: 8 September is RUOK? (Are You OK?) Day.[19] A gentle – and much-needed – reminder to people to check in with other humans and ask how they're doing in the hope that a conversation may help.

In all honesty, every day should be RUOK? Day in workplaces around the world and managers should be making a commitment to ensuring that people's stress levels are appropriate to produce great work, not great fear. During their lifetime, most people will spend more time with people at work than with those that they love and they don't want to spend that time in a never-ending pit of stress, anxiety or depression. Prolonged exposure to these kinds of working conditions can lead to long-term mental health issues and in some cases, even suicide.[20]

The pandemic has exacerbated these issues for many individuals, leading collaboration technology company Slack to find that anxiety and work-related stress are at an all-time high.[21] Yet, incredibly, there are managers in senior positions telling staff to 'suck it up', 'knuckle down and get on with it', 'just leave if you don't like it' or 'find ways to enjoy your job'. But this issue is not about leaving (someone else will merely step into that mess) or prolonged enjoyment, it's about humans being afraid. Afraid of making a mistake, afraid of making a decision, afraid to be honest, afraid to call out poor behaviour, afraid to say, 'hey, maybe we do have enough people, we just have too much work?'.

The consistent narrative is more, more, more. Can you cover an extra shift? Can you get me the report by 5 p.m.? Can you attend this meeting? Can you respond to my email by 12 p.m.? Can you deliver this by 6 a.m.? Acronyms such as ASAP and even JFDI are prevalent in workplaces around the world. As is the insidious concept of 'doing more, with less', which is simply not possible. Every time I hear a senior business leader utter those four words, a piece of every employee dies inside – they are a corporate Horcrux.[22] When they hear those words, employees know what it actually means – 'do more, later at night' – all of which leads to toxic productivity.

It's worth pointing out the difference between those who choose to work late at night and toxic productivity. The former is a choice that people make, usually based on their personal circumstances. It's part of their life 'balance'. I used to pick the kids up from school, spend time with them and then return to work at 5 p.m. This suited my lifestyle and the organization supported that, which was fantastic. But it was my choice and an agreement that I made with my employer. Or else, the former could also be a result of the fact that the individual is badly organized or chooses procrastination over productive work.

Toxic productivity occurs where your organization expects you to work longer hours because 'I want to see signs of your commitment to us', 'that's what someone in your role does' or 'because that's what I'm paying you to do'. Sometimes, it's all three! The goal for these kinds of organizations appears to be continual busyness. And for those stuck in that cycle at the minute it's worth reminding you of this statement, from UCLA Basketball Coach John Wooden, 'Never mistake activity for achievement.'

The word 'busy' is often worn as a badge of honour or else, people are afraid that if they're not *seen* as being busy all of the time, then it will compromise how they are thought of as an employee. Yet, this busyness is taking a terrible toll on their mental and physical health. According to the reports, almost 80 per cent of employees are experiencing some form of burnout at work, while for senior leaders, nearly 60 per cent felt completely used up by the end of their working days.[23]

Toxic productivity can also lead to hyper competitiveness in some workplaces, such as real estate, trading, retail and law. In these kinds of environments (and it's not limited to these), people compete with each other to be the busiest, best or simply to be seen as the person who solves the most complex problem or attracts the biggest client.

Data published by the *Financial Times* found that, in a survey of 2,000 lawyers, those 'who felt high levels of stress were 22x more prone to suicidal thoughts than their low-stress counterparts'.[24] Workplace stress can also lead to an increased dependency on drugs and alcohol.[25]

Toxic productivity is simply not sustainable. Judging people by how busy they are is an appalling practice, as is monitoring how long they are online or any other productivity tests, for that matter. And employees have frankly had enough of not having time to do their work. Especially given that only 12 per cent of employees believe that they can currently contribute six hours a day to their job.[26]

Toxic productivity hit the news in late 2022 when employees around the world decided not to do it anymore. The US-based movement became known as *quiet quitting*. It was characterized by employees doing only what was necessary to do their job and no more. As you'd expect there was a pile on from people with old-fashioned working attitudes, yet ultimately the movement was a rejection – by employees everywhere, of all ages – of toxic productivity.

I was interviewed about it at the time and was asked whether I supported the movement and my response to that question hasn't changed. If any organization or team works to build a culture of empathy and compassion that values prioritization, collaboration and discipline then people will always go the extra mile, when required to do so. If not, then they can expect active disengagement, which may ultimately lead to a toxic culture. It's not like the research isn't there to demonstrate what happens when you show empathy and care for others, and the benefits it provides. The Limeade Institute's Science of Care research[27] found that when employees feel cared for:

- Ninety per cent say they're likely to recommend their organization as a great place to work (compared to 9 per cent of those who don't feel cared for) – which leads to the retention of great people and the attraction of new ones.
- Ninety-four per cent say they feel personally engaged in their work (compared to 43 per cent of those who don't feel cared for) – leading to increased collaboration, productivity and innovation.
- Ninety-four per cent say they have well-being in their life (compared to 52 per cent of those who don't feel cared for) – leading to happy humans, the ultimate goal for every employer!

Shopify is a good example of an organization that leads by example (at time of writing, at least!). Back in December 2019, its CEO Tobi (Tobias) Lutke admitted on Twitter[28] that he doesn't overwork, ensures that he's present with his family at 5.30 p.m. every evening and wants his employees to do likewise.

He said, 'My belief is that there are five creative hours in everyone's day. All I ask of people at Shopify is that four of those are channelled into the company.' He went on to say, 'We don't burn out people. We give people space. We love real teams with real friendships forming.'

If the CEO of a $50bn global company can do this, then it's possible for others too.

Is technology a help or a hindrance?

There's a scene in the TV show *Succession* where the head of the (fictional) global TV news company ATN, Tom Wambsgans, is being grilled by a senate hearing into misconduct on one of the company's cruises. During the session we find out that Tom had sent his assistant Greg the exact same email 67 times, with the subject line 'You can't make a Tomelette without breaking some Greggs' and that the only time during the day when he didn't send the email was between the hours of 1 and 3 a.m.

It's a laugh-out-loud funny moment and yet, when I rewatched this particular scene, like much of the rest of the (brilliantly written) show, you can see that the scene is grounded in reality. Being swamped with passive-aggressive emails at all times of the day and night is a lived experience for many employees. So much so that France, Belgium, Italy, Slovakia, the Philippines and other countries have all implemented laws that prevent companies from contacting their employees outside working hours. These 'right to disconnect' laws are seen as necessary as companies around the world place undue pressure on employees to respond to emails, phone/video calls or any other electronic work-related tools outside working hours.

France is leading the way, with the law passing into force in January 2017 for companies of more than 50 employees.[29] Those with less than 50 employees are required to produce a document outlining their own rules for the use of digital tools. Employers who are found to have broken the law are liable to prosecution for 'obstructing the exercise of union rights' and the official found to be most accountable can be sent to prison for a year and given a €3,750 fine.

Of course, governments regulating every element of work isn't a good thing, so organizations should instead focus their efforts on the responsible use of technology such that it becomes a catalyst for productive work within working hours, not a barrier or distraction to the lives of its employees. And if there's one thing that technology has the capacity to do it's to distract employees from their work. Indeed, in one survey conducted by the Singapore University of Management, less than half the people they spoke to actually felt that they had the skills needed to use tools effectively.[30]

The average office worker gets notifications from an average of 6.2 applications per day.[31] One of these tools is email, estimated to be used by half the world's population (4bn people), who will send a total of almost 400bn emails per year by 2026.[32] A pretty ugly statistic, especially when you consider that – in my experience and that of my clients – most emails are generally sent for two reasons and two reasons alone: 1) so that people can cover their arse; 2) so that people can prove that they're smart.

Uffizi gallery director Eike Schmidt got so sick of people misusing email that he sent an email (I know…) to everyone, having a go at the way people write emails.[33] This was one of my favourite stories of the year as these things tend to remain in people's heads, not in the public domain. It was particularly focused on punctuation but I liked this line the most: 'Work emails should always be "clear, explicit and never allusive".' If only. In fact, I think many people send emails and electronic messages to be the opposite of this!

Of course, responsible use of technology is not limited to use of email, it also refers to the use of other applications too. Ex-president of the CBI Tony Danker – who was mired in a toxic culture crisis that brought into question the very existence of the organization (see Chapter 5: What do you value?) – confirmed in an interview with the BBC that he'd been fired for, among other things, viewing the Instagram accounts of staff and sending non-work related messages to staff on work messaging platforms.[34]

Danker – in the same interview – claimed to have been made the fall guy for the culture issues in the business, yet he appears never to have asked himself the question, 'Is it right for a president of a company to be viewing the Instagram pictures of younger members of staff and sending them messages about non-work related issues?'

I'll answer this question, just in case you're thinking that there's nothing wrong with this statement: 'Yes, it is wrong. It's a demonstration that you don't really understand how to use technology and honestly, you need a hobby if this is how you're planning to spend your time as a senior business leader.'

The British government is also under fire as I write – well, for many things – but let's limit it to this one thing for now: its use of WhatsApp groups. The use of WhatsApp groups is ubiquitous in Westminster and is used to connect ministerial groups, civil servants (i.e. government employees), individual ministers and of course, leaking stories to the press.[35] MPs have had to apologize for their behaviour on the app and despite end-to-end encryption, there are fears that people lurk within groups waiting to expose the latest foul-up to the public. And that's before you take into consideration that WhatsApp is owned by – and shares information with – Facebook. Yes, the messages themselves are secure, but that doesn't stop the app from accessing IP address, location, language, mobile phone network, browser details, time zone and more, then sending it back to Facebook to 'operate, provide, improve, understand, customize, support and market our services'. Ugh.[36]

The fact of the matter is most employees – and you may be one of them – simply don't know how to use technology to their advantage in the workplace. I'm not talking about the technical applications that surgeons, sports coaches, sales professionals, architects etc. use to enhance their work. Here, I mean the tools that you use that should aid collaboration: email, appointments, messaging, video conferencing, finance, performance tracking and so on. Very few, if any, organizations that I've worked with provide any kind of training on the cultural norms that exist to ensure that technology isn't used in a way that can give rise to toxic culture. You may have an acceptable use policy, however, that's a safety net or a protection mechanism when what's actually required is a charter for email use or better still, to be surrounded by people that use it responsibly.

Agreeing how technology will be used to collaborate effectively is vitally important. Younger members of staff will want to see technology embraced, given the digital nativity of their youth while at the same time, senior leaders will look to leverage it further to better deliver products, services, to reduce costs or to demonstrate their ability to maintain relevance in an ever changing world.

At present, only 30 per cent of employees, according to one Qualtrics survey in 2022, say that their experience with the technology that their company uses exceeds their expectations[37] and most will spend an average of 54 minutes a day dealing with technology challenges.[38] Yet when employees feel that they have technology that supports them to be productive at work, then they are 230 per cent more engaged and 85 per cent more likely to stay beyond three years.[39]

The respectful, sensible use of technology is critically important as a lever to mitigate the risk of collaboration and communication becoming toxic. Every organization should understand and actively promote the distinction between synchronous and asynchronous communication such that employees understand what's important and what's not. What requires an immediate response and what doesn't. And how to ensure that respect is maintained through messaging.

As Hollywood director Steven Spielberg once said, 'Technology can be our best friend, and technology can also be the biggest party pooper of our lives.'[40] Learning not to be a party pooper when using technology will always be time well spent.

Detox your culture: actions

Putting a group of people together, who understand each other's strengths and opportunities for improvement, isn't an antidote to toxic culture, in and of itself. Time needs to be taken to agree how you will work together to achieve success. This includes how you will behave, how you will hold each other accountable, how you will utilize technology, how you will maintain workplace safety and – if all that goes well – how you will celebrate success and take time out to recover so you can do it all again!

When teams don't take the time to agree how they'll work together then it will be almost impossible for them to work well with others too. This will give rise to silos (i.e. where teams can't work well with each other) and dramatically increases the possibility of these relationships becoming toxic and spreading throughout the organization.

Five things:

1. Spend time with your team to agree principles of how you'll work together.
2. Don't walk past poor behaviour, deal with it – or report it – immediately.
3. Measure how healthy and safe people feel in the company, rather than just how 'engaged' they are – and then act on the feedback, don't just report it.
4. Don't place undue pressure or demands on employees to work out of hours.
5. Implement a charter on how technology/tools will be used to improve collaboration and ensure senior managers role model this for others.

CHAPTER NINE

Are you standing still?

'Foregoing good culture is wiping companies' share prices and the value of their brand and their business overnight.'

Fiona Hathorn, CEO and Co-founder of Women on Boards[1]

Throughout all of the case studies that I've included in this book and the many stories that haven't made it, I find myself wondering – as you will have done too – 'why do people still think/act/behave in that way?'

I thoroughly enjoyed watching the 2023 Women's Soccer World Cup tournament. A fantastic month-long event that was equal parts dramatic, exciting and heartbreaking for most of the teams that took part. Ultimately, Spain were the winners, having played fantastically well to beat England in the final. The tournament did much to dispel myths surrounding women's football but also to elevate the progress made by these dedicated professionals, often in the face of continued sexism in the pubs, clubs, workplaces and institutions around the world. And while the media – for the most part – celebrated this evolution and championed the rise of the sport and the incredible potential for women's professional sports around the world, one story stuck out and continued to rumble on, months after the final.[2]

When the victorious Spanish team were celebrating on the podium post-match, the president of the Spanish Football Federation (effectively the organization that runs Spanish football), Luis Rubiales, who was on the podium as a guest of honour, tightly hugged forward Jenni Hermoso, grabbed her head and kissed her full on the lips.

Hermoso's immediate reaction after the celebration was to say via a livestream 'Eh, but I didn't like it!', before stepping back a little, saying that it was a 'natural gesture of affection' and that 'The President and I have a great relationship, his behaviour with all of us has been outstanding and it was a natural gesture of affection and gratitude.'

Rubiales formally apologized on the Monday following the final, saying, 'I have to apologize, I have no other choice. And also I can learn from this and need to understand that when you are the President of as important an institution as the Federation in ceremonies of this type you need to be more careful.'

Hmm, he started well with his apology and then it tailed off and became more about media and outside perception, rather than him understanding what it means to be respectful and being able to recognize and control his emotions.

A classic case of 'sorry, not sorry'.

When people around the world witnessed Rubiales' actions it left most of us wondering, 'why on earth did he think it was OK to do that?' It sends a message to those watching – particularly males – that this kind of behaviour is acceptable. But it's not and what's required – in order to maintain respect, dignity and safety for all in the workplace, even if it's on a football pitch – is for people to not only keep their emotions in check (emotions are often used as an excuse for harassment) but also to recognize what the world demands, in terms of behaviour, towards other humans.

This kind of behaviour should never have been acceptable; the fact that it became so is a failure of our society and workplaces in general. That said, people need to educate themselves accordingly to ensure that situations like this are never repeated 'in the heat of the moment'.

Rubiales initially tried to brush the whole thing off as something that people outside were more concerned about, calling them 'idiots and stupid people' before adding, 'Let's ignore them and enjoy the good things.'

Condemnation of his actions was swift. The players' union FIFPRO described his actions as 'not appropriate or acceptable in any context', while the acting Prime Minister of Spain, Pedro Sánchez, said, 'What we saw is unacceptable, and the apologies offered by Mr. Rubiales are not sufficient, I would call them inappropriate, so he must continue taking further steps to clarify what we all saw.'[3]

The Spanish Minister for Equality, Irene Montero,[4] described his actions as a 'form of sexual violence that we women suffer on a daily basis and until now has been invisible. We can't normalize this.'

She finishes by saying that it is the task of the whole society. While the Spanish society as a whole cannot be blamed for Rubiales' behaviour, Montero is right to suggest that it is likely a symptom of society. Spain has introduced new legislation aimed at evolving society to stop this kind of assault (an unsolicited kiss) happening anywhere, in the hope that behaviour in general will evolve to meet the standards expected of today.

Another example of this is to be found in the 2023 Baroness Casey review into the toxic workplace at the Metropolitan Police in London. She said, 'Views that the Met is "no worse than other organizations", or even other countries, and that sexist and misogynistic behaviours are a reflection of general society missed the point that more is expected of police officers.'

A recent research piece from MIT Sloan[5] found that women were 41 per cent more likely to experience a toxic culture than their male counterparts. What's interesting is that the results were skewed by the fact that toxic cultures were more prevalent in early education, health and beauty, nursing and social work – roles where women are more heavily represented. They further found that 'the toxic culture gap is correlated with the mix of male and female employees in an occupation.'

As attitudes change towards the treatment of different genders and races, and as industries broaden their talent pools to attract people previously underrepresented, societal shifts will affect how workplace cultures are understood, built and maintained. Therefore, one of the biggest challenges in avoiding (or addressing) a toxic workplace culture is in understanding how culture is built in the first place and the responsibility that organizations have in ensuring that they play a positive role in its evolution, both inside and outside the workplace.

It's not enough for organizations to simply say 'well, that's the way society is', they have to become role models for the society that they wish to see. In short, they cannot afford to stand still and let culture be done to them. In this scenario they will lose out on the people who want to be part of something different. Something humane, which addresses the perceived old-fashioned way of thinking and doing and paves the way for a better working future for all.

All talk, no behaviour change

Many organizations still seem to be great at talking about change but poor at executing it in a way that generates a sense of excitement around what's possible, ultimately leading to a vibrant culture.

Again, from the Baroness Casey review, 'We found no shortage of initiatives to address culture change in the Met, but these generated more activity than action.' Culture change or transformation initiatives and programs are routinely undertaken and mostly fail because:

a) organizations forget that cultures evolve over time, so these kinds of programs need to be continual, not have an end date;

b) they generate hours of activities involving operating model, process, structure and policy reviews but no meaningful actions to change the way things are done; or

c) the behaviour of individuals is never addressed, which in turn – *if done well* – will eventually lead to the positive evolution of culture and the maintenance or achievement of results.

All three of these issues are present in the report summarizing the toxic culture at the Metropolitan Police and so there can be little surprise that previous change efforts have failed. Baroness Casey called it 'Initiative-itis'. The new Met Police commissioner, Sir Mark Rowley (and all those who follow him), would do well to take heed of this if lasting culture change is the goal.

A recent example of transformation failure in the US is clothing retailer, Forever21.[6] Not only did the transformation itself fail, but it led to business failure.

Forever21 was founded in 1984 by Do Won Chang and Jin Sook Chang. It gained a massive following due to its rapidly changing inventory, low prices and ability to quickly respond to fashion trends. The stores offered a wide range of styles, catering to various tastes and preferences. By 2013 there were almost 500 stores, generating revenue of almost US$4bn. However, the brand faced criticism for its culture, labour practices and environmental impact. They also faced criticism for ignoring societal changes, famously hitting the media (social, then traditional) for sending out diet bars with plus-size orders.[7]

The financial woes of Forever21 started in 2017. Prior to that, the company had seen multimillion-dollar revenue since its creation in the mid-eighties. Revenue peaked at $4.4bn in 2015 and then the world started to change.

Regulators were examining the working practices of so-called 'fast-fashion' organizations and latterly, there was a demand from customers for the organization to become more sustainable. It also faced increased competition and it became apparent that it needed to change – and fast. However, they failed to implement new digital technology to improve the in-store or online experience, didn't embrace social media in the way that its competitors did and didn't do enough research before moving away from traditional revenue streams and going after business and floor space that wasn't suited to their model. All of which led to them filing for bankruptcy in September 2019, leading to the closure of 350 stores.

In a report, KPMG found[8] that only 20 per cent of organizations that they surveyed saw returns greater than 10 per cent from their transformation programs and that's if they ever got to the point where they were completed. And according to McKinsey, only 20 per cent of government transformations ever achieve their objectives.[9]

Interestingly, Capgemini undertook some research[10] to measure the effectiveness of digital transformation over a two-year period and found that the biggest barrier to transformation is the prevailing culture. What makes this interesting is that the thing being changed in a transformation program *is* the culture (digital refers to the tool or set of tools being implemented), so of course it'll be the biggest barrier to its own transformation! If it wasn't, there would be no need for a transformation program in the first place as employees would simply adopt the changes and work together to evolve the culture themselves.

They will do this if there is a continual investment in culture from the organization. They see the behaviours of leaders and the time and money being spent, not only in educating employees in different ways of thinking, acting and behaving, but also in celebrating the small wins and moments that for most, define their daily working lives. Unfortunately, organizations that do this are rare. When employees were asked by researchers what the reason was for their working culture being ineffective in practice, almost three quarters of respondents pointed to a lack of continual investment.[11]

A lack of money and time spent on culture is the perfect breeding ground for toxicity. It's a sure-fire way to demonstrate to employees that the leadership isn't interested in building or maintaining a culture that's fit for the future and that provides them with a pathway to improve their own skills and ultimately lives, through happiness, achievement, career progression, pay and benefits.

It is no secret that the organizations that are routinely voted as the best places to work continually invest in culture. They have a specific culture strategy that they execute every year and are at the forefront of not only building a place where people feel they can belong and contribute, but also contributes to the wider world too. These organizations seek to evolve ways of working by employing practices that people can take outside the workplace too.

The genesis of workplace culture

What this requires is an understanding of the mechanics of how workplace culture is built. Regardless of where you are in the world or what industry you work in, there are always three elements that contribute to the formation of a working culture. These are as follows:

Social Culture

Sociocultural anthropology, shortened to social culture here, is the study of traditions, customs, laws, politics, family structures, lived experiences, belief systems and gender studies in relation to global societal and cultural diversity. Through research, anthropologists are able to demonstrate 'that different people living in different environments will often have different cultures'. What this means for senior executives is that they need to understand the social conditions within which they operate.

In simple terms, it concerns understanding the culture within one's own country. However, many organizations now employ humans of all nationalities, whose lived social culture experiences are quite different from those within which they are working. These need to be factored into the working culture. Without an understanding of these differences, it's very easy for organizations to become drawn into the mistaken assumption that just because an organization is based in the UK (for example), then everyone understands the customs, beliefs and experiences of living there.

As a UK citizen myself, I understand that putting the kettle on and making a cup of tea is the answer to all of the world's problems (regardless of size or severity). However, this is not the case if you were born, raised or work in Ethiopia, Thailand, Denmark or Brazil!

Additionally, leaders also need to ensure that they retain a full awareness of what's happening within their social culture environment. This is important if they are to commit to a purpose that speaks to the 'way of the world' today.

When I first started work in 1987, very few – if any – organizations had an ESG (environmental, social and corporate governance) framework. That's simply unthinkable today and a demonstration that organizations have, as we say, 'moved with the times'.

People and Personality

While a key element of sociocultural anthropology is the study of humans, it's too simplistic to put all people from Japan, for example, in a box and say that they are the same based on where they were born. Yes, people are a product of their environment and their experiences (social culture), however, they are also unique and have a personality that is agnostic of that. This personality contains a set of strengths and opportunities for improvement, such that even twins who are biologically identical in almost every way may have completely different preferences.

Personality relates to the interrelationship between emotional, cognitive and behavioural patterns brought about by environmental and biological patterns. These 'strengths' are considered to be predominantly stable, yet do change over the course of our lives. As humans mature, we become more aware of our preferences and it's this self-awareness that helps us to build relationships with other humans and drives our curiosity towards the people and things that interest us.

Of course, many personality profiles attempt to categorize people – you're an extrovert, you're an introvert and so on – when the reality is we have a mix of preferences that we can bring to the fore at any given moment depending on how safe or stressed we feel at any given time.

According to researchers Hogan and Kaiser,[12] personality dictates leadership style, leadership style predicts employee attitudes and team functioning; and attitudes and team functioning predict organizational performance. Given that leadership is a choice (not necessarily a hierarchical position), people and their personality mix have a crucial role to play in the continual evolution of the sociocultural environment in which they're born, but also in the establishment of the working culture where they will collaborate with others to deliver successful outcomes.

Purpose, Vision and Values

As I discussed earlier in this book, every organization, regardless of location, industry or sector, has a reason for existing. An aspiration that it seeks to achieve and a set of morals that it expects of its employees in pursuit of aspiration achievement. In other words, purpose, vision and values. All of these attributes are extremely important inputs into the definition of workplace culture.

Purpose signals that the organization is in tune with the world (and social culture) in which it operates and demonstrates that the business has something to contribute to it.

Vision is a description of the aspiration that it has. This is an expectation of stakeholders, shareholders and potential employees that may wish to invest their time, money or career development in the organization. It has to be achievable for it to be believable and is set in line with strategy.

Values, meanwhile, are the organization's opportunity to make public the kind of environment that it seeks to build. Values summarize the emotional connections expected between employees and their work. They are translated into meaningful actions that people take every day.

These attributes are not only responsible for attracting people to the organization in the first place, but also in retaining high-potential employees and staying in step with global expectations. Unfortunately, when these cultural attributes are tested, they are often found to be wanting and the view from the outside is that the culture is therefore toxic. This affects not only the share price, but an organization's ability to attract the very people that it needs in order to address the challenges that it has. The model for workplace culture, therefore, looks like this:

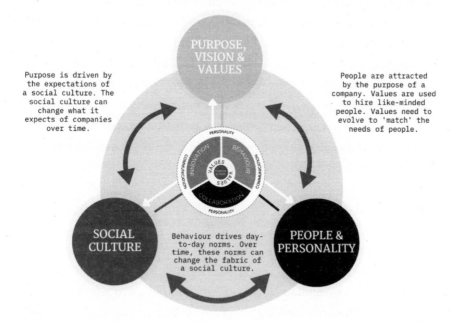

Purpose is driven by the expectations of a social culture. The social culture can change what it expects of companies over time.

People are attracted by the purpose of a company. Values are used to hire like-minded people. Values need to evolve to 'match' the needs of people.

Behaviour drives day-to-day norms. Over time, these norms can change the fabric of a social culture.

Organizations need to consider not only the social culture conditions within which they operate, but also give thought to the people that they are looking to attract. They need to deliberately define a purpose, vision and values that are not only in tune with the way of the world, but also make a statement of the standards that they hold to be true.

People are attracted to work for organizations where they believe there is a values match. And this values match is only possible if candidates see that the organization is relevant in the current global or national climate.

Global organizations (that is, those with subsidiaries around the world) need to be mindful of not imposing the 'head office' culture on each country. As this model demonstrates, only the purpose, vision and values should be shared and each country manager should be empowered to build their own working culture that aligns with the shared considerations. All three of these elements: social culture, people and personality, purpose, vision and values, combine to drive the deliberate definition of working culture.

In many ways, what this model highlights is the challenge that organizations who don't invest in culture continually face. The challenge of building something that is fit for purpose today that attracts the kinds of people that they need to maintain the results expected by shareholders or the general public. In not addressing this challenge, organizations will root themselves in a past that people don't wish to be part of and either choose not to apply, make noises during their employment or else continually leave.

Hybrid, AI and beyond

There's no greater example of this model than hybrid working, which rose to prominence post the COVID-pandemic and even now as I write this, continues to be a battleground between employers and employees. But before talking more about hybrid working, it's worth pointing out that 80 per cent[13] of the world's workforce aren't able to do it. They work in gardens, hospitals and sports teams. They fly planes, collect trash and build skyscrapers. They act in shows, deliver food or drive public transport. I think this statistic continually gets overlooked when organizations are looking to offer more flexibility for those that work in offices. In a recent speech to blue-collar workers, I referred to hybrid work as the new office privilege. Which, of course, it is.

There seem to be a high number of knowledge or other desk-bound workers demanding the right to be able to choose where they can work and when. This approach not only lacks empathy for those who aren't able to work more flexibly, but also assumes that the collaboration centres on the individual's needs, not those of the team.

For organizations with a mixed location workforce (as distinct from a geographically dispersed workforce), moving to a hybrid model is more complex. It requires good planning, participation from employees in all areas of the company and exemplary communication. Yet all too frequently, senior executives get it wrong and create tensions between those that can and those that can't, leading to a sense of inequity and/or not being listened to. And that's before you factor in the emotional and organizational maturity required to move to a model offering greater location flexibility for office workers. While 82 per cent[14] of employees may say that flexibility has made them happier, only 22 per cent of those say that their mental health has improved, 55 per cent say that micro-management has increased and a paltry 12 per cent[15] say that they are fully productive!

The empathy between workers that was evident during lockdowns has gradually ebbed away as people – noticing the change in social culture that led to remote working becoming more acceptable – have started to demand greater flexibility and that their needs are prioritized, rather than the requirements of the team. In this scenario, the opportunity for toxic culture is heightened and executives need to be mindful of their messaging in order to ensure that collaboration is maintained and that special circumstances aren't granted to one or two (or more!) individuals. They also need to educate themselves on what's possible to ensure that they don't become the firelighter, which is exactly what we saw as people started to resurface once lockdowns ended.

David Solomon from Goldman Sachs was one of the first to express his disdain for remote working: '[Remote work is] an aberration that we are going to correct as quickly as possible.'[16] He also made comments around remote working being bad for graduate learning, which I agreed with, but did he have to be so vehemently against the *notion* of remote work, especially as the shift had only just occurred in early 2021?

Solomon was closely followed by Bob Iger, CEO of Disney, who said, 'It is my belief that working together more in-person will benefit the company's creativity, culture, and our employees' careers.'[17] He said this in a memo to all staff, ordering them back to the office four days per week.

Disney's employees responded by creating a petition that gained over 2,500 signatures, arguing that the requirement was 'likely to have unintended consequences that cause long-term harm to the company by forcing out hard to replace talent'.[18]

Netflix, who are often seen as having one of the better workplace cultures (in the past at least), were also thrust into the limelight in 2020 when Founder and CEO Reed Hastings was interviewed by the *Wall Street Journal*.

'I don't see any positives (to working from home),' Hastings told the *Journal*. 'Not being able to get together in person, particularly internationally, is a pure negative.'[19]

The statistics are often contradictory as to the merits of face-to-face vs in-person interactions, which is why a mix of locations is definitely the best option, while organizations seek to find the perfect mix.

Of course, each of these senior leaders will have cut their teeth in an office and that will have shaped their view of how work should be done. However, it ignores the social culture shift in attitudes towards desk-based work. Taking a definitive stance of being for or against a change in working conditions is always going to create divisions. A better approach – one that would have lessened the opportunity of toxicity – would have been to take the time to work with employees on experimenting with different ways of working as well as upskilling managers on how to lead remote teams, to better understand how empathy, camaraderie and performance can be maintained, regardless of where someone is sat.

In my experience and through research for this book, where there is a simple concept to follow that may (or may not) impact culture, organizations are eager to follow suit. Some examples include:

- Implementing open-plan offices – which are proven to decrease, not increase, collaboration by 73 per cent![20] They also assume that everyone works in exactly the same way, which of course, they don't.

- Training everyone on diversity and inclusion – a noble concept, yet studies show that 'force-feeding can activate bias rather than stamp it out,'[21] leading to less diversity and inclusion.
- Making new hires undertake a psychological test – while this is often important for public safety positions, it won't ever identify whether the person is a good human and a good team player.
- Going agile – the entire world was going to be 'more agile' before the COVID-19 pandemic without asking themselves whether it was a good fit for their business. It was mostly used as an excuse to shortcut self-imposed bureaucracy.

On the face of it, simple approaches often appear easy to copy. The reality is that you can't copy culture and senior executives would do well to remember this. That said, inspiration can be taken from the work that others are doing to ensure that their cultures are evolving positively and actively looking to the future to embrace what's ahead.

And what's immediately ahead as I write this is the rise of Artificial Intelligence (AI for short). As early as 2018, Sundar Pichai, CEO of Google, said of AI, 'We recognize that such powerful technology raises equally powerful questions about its use. How AI is developed and used will have a significant impact on society for many years to come.'[22] He also said that AI is more profound than fire or electricity.[23]

Executives have a choice: a) be curious about how AI can improve their business and educate their employees, so that they can better understand the cultural shifts required; or b) stick their fingers in the ears and shout 'LALALALALA' loudly in the hope that it goes away or some new workplace fad replaces it.

Which would you choose?

If the COVID-19 pandemic response is anything to go by, then you can expect short-term, often rash, decisions that don't take the future into consideration. Jobs will be removed in the hope that AI can replace people and thus improve the bottom line. Or else organizations will waste millions on tools that they'll never use, just so that they can say they're an 'AI-first organization' or some other BS like that.

According to the Organization for Economic Cooperation and Development (OECD), the occupations at the highest risk from AI-driven automation are those that require highly-skilled people (particularly in the fields of law, culture and science), which according to their statistics is just over a quarter of employees across its 38 member countries.[24] They went on to say that, 'Urgent action is required to make sure AI is used responsibly and in a trustworthy way in the workplace.'

The fundamental concept underlying AI is straightforward: within a conventional software framework, an algorithm (or sequence of operations) is developed by a software engineer. Subsequently, this software is employed by users to streamline various tasks. As users interact with the software, they generate information. This information, constituting the outcomes or products of different operational activities (such as processing payroll, a prospective candidate submitting a job application, an employee enrolling in a course and so forth) is archived. Consequently, the software generates data as its user base continues to expand and its intelligence on how to answer queries increases.

AI essentially creates models. The models collect information and then the information can be used to inform decision-making. Therefore, if you wanted to assess the issues that could cause your culture to be toxic, you would need regular surveys to capture employees' comments. An AI model would then use this database of information to learn all about the culture and then provide analysis – at any time – on the risks faced without you ever having to print off a 30-page employee engagement report.

Goldman Sachs, in a report entitled 'The Potentially Large Effects of Artificial Intelligence on Economic Growth' (Briggs/Kodnani)[25] estimate that 300 million white-collar jobs could be affected.

CEOs are rushing to tell the world about their plans to leverage AI. When interviewed by Bloomberg News, the CEO of IBM, Arvind

Krishna, estimated that 7,800 jobs could be lost,[26] largely in the 'back office'.[27] However, unless we manage the integration of AI into our working cultures in a way that aids productivity, it will simply increase the opportunity for toxicity. Bots will run meetings, scan emails, predict behaviour, generate communication and the lines between humanity and technology will become even more blurred than they are now, with people's time being consumed by the complicated tools that they use (or the way that they use them), not the work that they do.

Executive Director of the Institute for the Future, Marina Gorbis, had this to say: 'Every time we program our environments, we end up programming ourselves and our interactions. Humans have to become more standardized, removing serendipity and ambiguity from our interactions. And this ambiguity and complexity is what is the essence of being human.'

For the last 20 years, organizations have looked to technology to aid the way that they work in the hope of improving productivity. Unfortunately, for most, the biggest challenges still appear to be emails and diary management. Which is why those that understand data are putting their faith in AI, not humans. But that's not to say that it's a good idea for everything.

Whilst writing this book, a writers' and actors' strike was underway in Hollywood. A strike is often the last resort for employees to express their dissatisfaction with the cultural conditions being offered by their employer. Basically, things need to be pretty bad for people to protest about culture in the streets.

The strike was predominantly about pay and financial security. And if you think everyone on strike gets a fair wage, think again. Valentina Garza, writer on the streaming show, *Jane the Virgin*, shared on Twitter a residual (i.e. a fixed amount not tied to viewer numbers) paycheque she received for writing two episodes. It was for 0.03 cents.[28]

There was also another element to the strike and that's the role of AI. Technology companies (of course!) have sold AI to the studios and production companies as *the future*, in the hope that they'll invest billions of dollars in their tools. Of course, the future they sell is the automation of the mundane and often time-consuming processes that lengthen film and TV show production. However, there are other processes apparently being (nefariously) considered for AI use, nefariously, by studio bosses. From replacing traditional artists to writing scripts to using actors' images to star in movies.[29]

You might be forgiven for thinking that it sounds like some future fanciful movie in and of itself, but the technology is already here. The writers and actors were right to voice their concerns about the use of AI (and their ownership of intellectual property and identity rights), given that it is already on their doorstep and thankfully they were able to come to an amicable agreement. Other industries should take note. Unless organizations agree humane standards on how AI will be employed and governed, the writers' and actors' strike will likely be the first of many as workers look to protect their rights, jobs and livelihoods. Any other approach will lead to toxicity, unwanted media coverage and an unavoidable impact on reputation and results.

Evolutionary education

Hybrid working, AI and whatever comes next are all things that need to be considered by organizations as they plan the evolutionary education of their management team. In his 2017 book, *Homo Deus: A Brief History of Tomorrow*, author Yuval Noah Harari said this, 'Very soon, the traditional model [of working] will become obsolete and the only way for humans to stay in the game will be to keep learning throughout their lives and reinvent themselves repeatedly.'

This moment has already arrived. That's not to say that everyone's job around the world has changed, it's just that the expectations that employees have about working conditions and culture have changed and organizations need to catch up.

There was a time, not so very long ago, when organizations would send people on endless classroom courses in the hope of changing their cultures, but I spoke to a client recently and when I asked her what needed to change, she said, 'We need to be more honest with each other.' She continued, 'We all went on a four-day leadership development program, but nothing has changed.'

A number of years ago, McKinsey analysed leadership development programs and found that only 6 per cent were considered to be successful, despite over US$14bn being spent on them every year.[30]

Many leadership development programs still take an old-fashioned classroom approach to training that often resembles a scene from the BBC TV show, *The Office*. Full of dated team-building exercises involving spaghetti and Blu-tack or being told to build structures from LEGO.

Now, if you work for LEGO, the latter is a great way to familiarize yourself with the product. However, employees today are looking for skills that they can immediately apply, delivered in a way that provides an experience rather than formal structures involving text books that people will never read.

By providing employees, but particularly managers, with short micro-learning experiences that involve accountability, organizations can transform the way that they not only develop their people, but also respond to the changing nature of their business. Yet, many reviews into toxic workplace cultures fail to adequately address this issue, which often demonstrates their own lack of understanding of the mechanics of culture and how skills need to consistently evolve.

A survey commissioned by insurance group Allianz[31] found that only 38 per cent of millennials believe their leader is skilled at responding to changing circumstances, which was the behaviour that they valued the most. Whereas 65 per cent of respondents in a survey by Deloitte[32] said that their organization had no program in place to instil the different behaviours and skills required for the digital age. Despite the world being in the 'digital age' for about 20 years now.

A survey from McKinsey,[33] undertaken post-pandemic, found that the expectations that employees have of managers had changed quite dramatically, from technical skills to emotional skills. This is a demonstration not only of how social cultures are changing, but also the value that employees now place on emotional intelligence, which for too long was seen as 'soft' or 'fluffy' skills. They want less 'showing operational excellence', 'establishing performance contracts' and 'focusing on competitive insights' and they want more 'Being supportive and caring', 'Being employee focused' and 'Being creative and entrepreneurial'. The latter requires the very thing that most people in non-vibrant cultures seem to be short of these days: time. When time is provided for employees to think and when they have the discipline to remove distractions, then the conditions for creativity exist.

In his book, simply titled *Creativity*, author John Cleese suggests that too often creativity is seen as a formal exercise within a business – 'we need to be creative!' – rather than something that people have time to spontaneously do. He suggests that creativity should be approached as a child would approach play: 'Children at play are totally spontaneous. They are not trying to avoid making mistakes. They don't observe rules.'

Creativity is only possible if people are prepared to challenge the status quo, the culture feels safe enough to do so and employees are provided with the time in which to do it. When the latter occurs, employees repay the trust with a change in behaviour and a desire to be part of an exciting – and evolutionary – future, where creative ideas can be implemented and become innovation. However, when the culture is stuck in a mode of permanent busyness, then people will disengage and tell each other what's *not* possible rather than what *is*.

Some simple rules for creative work include:

- No bad ideas
- No harmony
- No boring exercises
- No dull workspaces
- No implementation excuses

- No undue interference
- No idea too big
- No blame
- No opt-outs
- No end to it!

Inadequate education and a lack of creativity are two reasons why cultures don't evolve positively and why good people eventually leave. They want something different; something fresh, new, and that they can immediately put into practice. They want to feel inspired and motivated by the programs provided, as they would (say) watching a TED Talk. An hour on the value of AI, how to have courageous conversations, understanding different generations, how to set expectations, how to actively listen, how to reduce email and so on. By creating a culture evolution development plan organizations can get 5 per cent better each month, rather than expecting a 60 per cent jump after a single four-day program.

Detox your culture: actions

Cultures evolve, they don't change overnight. No amount of initiatives designed to address culture will ever be able to beat managing out a poorly-behaving or performing employee. Having said that, senior leaders need to understand the social context within which they are working and then never take their eye off it, to ensure that it remains continually fit for purpose to deliver the strategy that it has. This means constructing evolution plans that provide employees with things they can immediately do differently, delivered in a way that they'll never forget. Competition for human attention is greater today than it's ever been, but employees will always be engaged with approaches that provide them with immediate value.

Five things:

1. Beware of 'initiative-itis' where endless projects are created to address issues with the culture.
2. Stay attuned to what's happening in the world and how it may affect internal dynamics.
3. Don't dismiss or ignore new ways of doing things – ask yourself how they could add value to the way that you work.
4. Construct full-year micro-learning experiences to provide employees with the skills they need right now.
5. Provide employees with the time to think creatively and support efforts to implement those ideas. It will spark the innovation required to keep cultures relevant.

CHAPTER TEN

How will you respond?

'NEC must be confident that actions taken in the light of [the]
findings and recommendations will be effective in enabling
permanent, non-reversible measures to detoxify a culture of
harassment, bullying and misogyny.'

Prosiect Pawb (Everyone's Project)
review into Plaid Cymru toxic culture[1]

In many respects Anita Hill was the first.[*]

In 1991 she sat in front of a US Supreme Court nominee hearing to fulfil what she would later call her 'ethical responsibility to come forward in the best way and the most effective way that I could'. She alleged that Supreme Court nominee Clarence Thomas had sexually harassed her in the workplace when she reported to him at the Equality Opportunities Commission. As a result, she didn't feel he was fit to take up the role of Supreme Court judge.

Thomas denied the allegations and claimed that he was a victim of a 'high-tech lynching', an inflammatory reference to when African-Americans were accused of sexual misconduct prior to being lynched.

---

[*] It's worth also giving a mention to movies such as *Silkwood* (1983), *Serpico* (1973) and *Norma Rae* (1979). Each one told stories that were based on real-life events about harassment, corruption and the mistreatment of employees within workplaces in the 1960s and 1970s. However, given the fact that they were dramatizations of real events, none really ignited meaningful and lasting debate about how workers are treated.

(Hill is African-American, as is Thomas.) His impassioned plea gained him support throughout the country.

For her part, Hill was grilled about the allegation by 14 white men[2] in a very public hearing. There were others who also made allegations about Thomas and the culture that he presided over. However, seeing the treatment that Hill received from the panel, they declined to testify or else were never called.

The committee eventually sided with Thomas and deemed him fit for office.

As a result of the claims, Hill received bomb warnings, death threats and was left feeling isolated, both personally and professionally. Yet, in an interview in 2021, she said that she wouldn't change a thing as she was also inundated with messages of support and stories from others who had had similar experiences. She said, 'Hearing from them, just realizing that I was not alone in facing this kind of scrutiny and actual hostility, was affirming.'[3]

Seeing Hill lay bare her emotions about the conduct she'd witnessed emboldened others in US and global workplaces. In the US alone, changes to workplace practices that can be directly linked back to the courage that Hill showed are as follows:

1. Awareness and Sensitivity: The controversy brought widespread attention to the issue of sexual harassment in the workplace. It raised awareness about the prevalence of such behaviour and highlighted the importance of addressing it. Many employers and employees became more sensitive to the issue and began taking steps to prevent and respond to sexual harassment.

2. Legal Changes: The controversy played a role in prompting discussions about strengthening laws related to workplace harassment and discrimination. The Civil Rights Act of 1964[4] had already prohibited workplace discrimination on the basis of sex, but the controversy led to increased scrutiny of these laws and discussions about potential amendments.

3. Civil Rights Act Amendments: In 1991, following the Anita Hill hearings, Congress passed the Civil Rights Act of 1991.[5] This act made several important changes to existing civil rights laws, including those related to workplace discrimination. Notably, it allowed for the recovery of compensatory and punitive damages in cases of intentional employment discrimination, including cases involving sexual harassment. Previously, only back pay and injunctive relief were available as remedies.

4. Burden of Proof: The Civil Rights Act of 1991 also shifted the burden of proof in discrimination cases.[6] Before this act, employees had the burden of proving that discrimination was a motivating factor in an adverse employment action. The 1991 amendments lowered this burden, making it easier for employees to prove their claims.

5. Training and Education: The Anita Hill controversy led many employers to recognize the need for training and education on preventing sexual harassment in the workplace. Many companies began implementing formal sexual harassment training programs for their employees, which aimed to create a more inclusive and respectful workplace environment.

6. EEOC Enforcement: The Equal Employment Opportunity Commission (EEOC), the federal agency responsible for enforcing workplace discrimination laws, also saw an increase in complaints related to sexual harassment following the Anita Hill controversy.[7] This highlighted the need for the EEOC to take these complaints seriously and to provide clear guidance to employers and employees on addressing harassment.

7. Corporate Policies: Many companies updated their policies and procedures for addressing workplace harassment and discrimination. They developed clearer guidelines for reporting incidents, investigating complaints and taking appropriate corrective actions.

8. Cultural Impact: The controversy and subsequent discussions had a broader cultural impact, leading to conversations about gender dynamics, power imbalances and the treatment of women in various

industries. It paved the way for more open conversations about these issues and contributed to changing societal attitudes that continue to this day.

Overall, while Hill's allegations didn't directly result in new laws, they played a pivotal role in pushing conversations about workplace harassment and discrimination to the forefront. The legal changes that did occur were largely aimed at strengthening existing laws and providing better remedies for victims of workplace discrimination.

Like I said, in many ways Hill was the first to bring an allegation of this kind of inappropriate workplace behaviour and culture into the public domain. Unfortunately, however, she won't be the last. But, how do you know that your workplace is toxic?

Spotting the signs

Throughout the course of this book, I've provided endless examples and case studies of signs that were missed by organizations or else they chose to ignore. Almost all of the instances of toxic culture described here were avoidable through early detection and decisive action.

True, there were some that failed to make it high enough such that leaders could take meaningful action. For example, the Fox Williams report into the Confederation of British Industry 'did not hear evidence or receive information that demonstrates that the senior leadership within the CBI had any awareness of the allegations made prior to their publication'.[8] This, of course, presents its own problems as – given the allegations of rape, sexual assault and inappropriate behaviour – they really should have known and the HR department was found to be culpable in its consistency of reporting upwards to the board.

Unfortunately, however, the review then failed to insist on more direct communication of potential future issues, suggesting instead that the CBI just 'consider [my emphasis] introducing a process/protocol for escalating and dealing with complaints about Board members, including the President' rather than insisting on it.

There is simply no excuse for all levels of leadership not to be made aware of allegations of toxic culture. I'm not advocating for the board of directors to be informed of combatant cultures where individuals may be being performance managed, or else the communication of team members isn't as appropriate as it could be for work to get done. However, as soon as any alleged poor behaviour or maltreatment is reported, then all levels of senior leadership need to be advised and a plan to address the allegations put into action.

Boards cannot simply put reports of toxic culture in a box and bury them in the garden in the hope that people don't see them or forget that the incident(s) occurred in the first place. They need to ensure that action is taken by those who have responsibility for them.

A report from Ernst & Young[9] found that '27 per cent of boards never or rarely discuss the culture needed to support organizational strategy' and that is unacceptable. If the board is concerned about results, then they need to also be concerned about *how* those results are to be achieved. As the report also said, 'Boards that overlook corporate culture can put their organizations at risk.'

Better still would be to get an employee voice on culture onto boards. Not only will this provide a unique insight into the culture 'on the shop floor', it will also provide boards with the mechanism to identify and address possible activism by employees in relation to the culture.

According to a survey by the law firm Herbert Smith Freehills,[10] employee activism could cost organizations up to 25 per cent of their global revenue each year due to the disruptive nature of strikes and reputational damage leading to lost business. Saying you stand for one thing and acting another way is one of the fastest ways companies can erode trust with employees. It also looks really bad to customers.

Instead of fearing employee activism, this is an opportunity for boards to empower their people and demonstrate to staff, stakeholders and customers that they stand for something, with actions behind the words. Keeping employee activism outside of the boardroom creates division and can even end up pitting employees against management.

As Fiona Hathorn, Chief Executive and co-founder of Women on Boards, said, 'Companies really need to think of how they get the voice of the employee in the boardroom.'[11]

Hearing this voice may also mitigate the risks of the organization opening itself up to criticism via social media on X (formerly Twitter) accounts such as @fuckyouiquit. @PayGapApp is another example of how social media is being used to expose organizations that say one thing, but do another.

The creator of the Gender Pay Gap Bot – Francesca Lawson[12] – had simply had enough of seeing bland marketing statements put out by communications departments about equality, despite them failing to take meaningful action to address it. So she created a bot that uses freely available pay data published by companies (in the UK) to highlight where those companies who tweet about International Women's Day have a disparity between the pay of females and males.

Senior leaders – including boards – *must* take an active interest in the culture of the organization and include it as a measure of CEO performance. The UK Corporate Governance Code insists on this approach, saying: 'The board should assess and monitor culture. Where it is not satisfied that policy, practices or behaviour throughout the business are aligned with the company's purpose, values and strategy, it should seek assurance that management has taken corrective action.'[13]

While the UK code states this, it is still not common practice. One report[14] found that while almost three quarters of auditors said their boards had taken an active interest in the culture, more than half had never been asked to provide reports on it, so they could assess its health and whether action is required. 37 per cent do not formally assess culture at all.

Surveys, pulse checks and reports

Reports and employee surveys are the most popular way for companies to gauge culture and to uncover potential issues that need to be addressed. The oft-reviled 'Engagement Survey' has a chequered history, yet when done well can provide organizations and their leaders with insights upon which they can immediately act on.

Management theories began shifting towards valuing employee satisfaction and motivation in the 1930s. The Human Relations Movement[15] – born out of the Hawthorne studies[16] in the 1920s – emphasized the importance of psychological and social factors in the workplace. By the 1970s – and fuelled by The Quality of Work Life[17] movement – employee surveys had become a staple in many of the large organizations and they focused largely on job satisfaction, communication and working conditions.

By the 2000s, technology had replaced the paper-based approach and simplified the process of gathering information and by the 2010s, workplaces started to introduce 'Pulse' surveys. Pulse surveys were a way of moving away from the once-a-year approach to provide richer data on culture and also to ensure that issues were being picked up sooner rather than later.

With advancements in artificial intelligence and data analytics, organizations are now exploring ways to use predictive models to anticipate employee needs, predict turnover and proactively address potential issues. Yet, any information collected or predicted is only as good as the action it initiates. I spoke with an employee recently and asked whether she'd responded to the recent engagement survey that her organization had undertaken. She rolled her eyes (never a good sign) and said that she had wasted 20 minutes(!) answering questions. When I asked her why this was a waste, she said, 'Because they never do anything with the information anyway.' Unfortunately, this is the lived experience of many employees.

Valuable productive time spent providing honest insights into what's good and what's not in order to produce a report that few people read, and a list of actions that the organization never follows through on, in any meaningful way. At that point, many employees will turn to Glassdoor and leave their review and feedback there.

Glassdoor is an American-based website where employees can leave reviews on the culture of their company. Founded in 2007, its popularity has grown ever since. In 2015, Glassdoor in the UK was regarded by those that used it as a more trustworthy source of information than career guides or official company web pages and documents.[18] That said, in 2022, New Zealand-based toy company ZURU sued Glassdoor[19] as they alleged that 'false, disparaging and defamatory' reviews had harmed its business and reputation, leading to issues with hiring new staff. Anonymous reviewers had left comments about ZURU on Glassdoor, calling it a 'burnout factory' with 'incompetent leaders' who presided over a 'toxic culture'.

A Californian court ruled in favour of ZURU and ordered Glassdoor to reveal the identities of the people that left the reviews. Judge Tse wrote,[20] 'Glassdoor wants to safeguard anonymous speech on its website. ZURU wants to protect its reputation. Both interests can't simultaneously be accommodated.'

However, lawyers see this as a bad thing as it impinges on individuals' right to free speech.[21] It's a complicated issue for lawmakers to assess. However, it wouldn't be as much of a concern to organizations if they put time, money and thought into their cultures in the first place or else acted on the feedback that employees provide.

Employee listening tools can be a great way for companies to understand and enhance the employee experience in the workplace. However, the following principles should be taken into consideration when using them:

- Little and often – focus on fewer questions that provide easy-to-interpret information at more regular intervals throughout the year
- Employee view – ask the questions from the perspective of the employee ('Do you see our values being consistently practised by our leadership

team?') rather than the employer ('Do you understand how to put the values into practice?')

- Don't keep asking the same people – vary the people that you ask so that they don't get survey fatigue
- Create safety – give employees the option to provide their name if they wish to do so. They are less likely to do this in a toxic culture, hence why anonymity should be offered.

I've included that last point because it's important to hear all voices. However, it's a complete failure of leadership if anonymity or whistleblowing is the only way people feel comfortable providing feedback on what they perceive to be wrong with the organization.

Once the information has been collected and distilled into key themes, then an action plan should be created and senior leadership owners identified for each one. Action should be taken within the first one to three months of the feedback being provided and any signs of toxicity immediately escalated for investigation. Leaders should be measured on their delivery to the culture actions by way of demonstrating to staff that their feedback has not been in vain, with the ultimate objective being that the culture improves.

Organizations will often focus on the score, which provides evidence – at the point when the survey was conducted – of how employees view the culture. It's helpful to be able to view the score at a team level, as often it's not clear where the issues – or high-potential people – exist. The score can then be used the following year to measure whether improvements have been made or not. If the score goes up, leaders should continue to invest in culture and thus will see continual improvement. But if the score goes down, leaders may need to be replaced as clearly progress isn't being made.

I'm often asked for my view on 'the score' and my answer has always been the same: it's not the score that's important, it's the feedback behind it that is.

Another question I'm asked is whose responsibility is it to collect this information? That's a slightly more controversial answer. If you have an internal audit department, it should be their responsibility to run the engagement survey. If not, then it should reside with your HR/ People and Culture department.

This is an unpopular opinion with the HR folk, as they've done it forever and see culture as their responsibility. However, there are three good reasons why audit should take responsibility for this:

1. Independence – management, employees and external parties, like shareholders or regulators, are more likely to trust the results of an audit conducted by independent professionals. Audit can present an unbiased view of the findings and help to identify any risks as a result of the feedback provided. Independence is closely linked to maintaining ethical standards (see below) and professional integrity. Without independence, there's a risk of compromising values and engaging in practices that may harm the organization in the long run.

2. Better understanding of the law/ethics – Internal audit's role is to safeguard the integrity of the organization's culture, operations, promote compliance with legal and regulatory requirements, and ensure that the company's reputation remains untarnished. By monitoring ethical behaviour, internal auditors can help prevent instances of fraud, corruption and misconduct or any other activity that undermines the safety within the culture. They can also recommend actions that need to be taken to address instances where they believe ethics and standards have been compromised.

3. Don't 'protect' senior leaders – closely linked to their independence, auditors ignore organizational hierarchies and focus purely on the actions of others. These include governance activities as well as individuals' behaviours and team dynamics, which may or may not be driven by leadership. Treating leaders differently from other employees when it comes to presenting feedback from an engagement

survey can create an atmosphere of inequality and favouritism. This can lead to resentment among employees, erode morale and negatively impact the overall work culture. Treating everyone equally in terms of accountability promotes a sense of fairness and equity within the organization and audit are best placed to do this as they should be operating without allegiances.

4. HR can often be part of the problem – HR don't own culture, they're part of it, just like everyone else. Yes, they have responsibility for building a culture strategy and for constructing a learning and development program that ensures that managers and staff have the skills to be able to build and evolve culture. However, they should also be treated the same as every other department and it's hard to retain objectivity when the feedback is often directed at the people running the survey. It could also be the case in your organization that HR don't *actually* understand culture and this can be drawn out of the survey by auditors simply looking to establish the facts about the culture and where it's at, at that time.

Toxic culture *mea culpas*

As you have seen throughout this book, instances where senior leaders are not aware of toxic culture issues are few and far between. Almost every reported instance makes it to a manager, who reports it to another manager in the hope that something will get done.

Whether the issue(s) affects performance, leads to the resignation of staff or makes it into the media will largely depend on the organization's response. Some organizations and individuals simply choose to dismiss the allegations out of hand and make matters a whole lot worse than they were before. Ladies and gentlemen, the Spanish Football Federation…

Not only did they choose to support embattled head Luis Rubiales (*see also* p. 144) by allowing him to keep his job following the 'sexual violence' he inflicted upon player Jenni Hermoso, they then doubled down, stating that they intend to take Hermoso to court for lying! And people (mainly men) wonder why more women don't speak out about the injustices they face in the workplace?

Things became so bad that the Spanish government intervened and when toxic culture becomes political, this will magnify the issues tenfold. Politicians love to give private business a kicking as there really is no downside for them.

And politicians have been able to put the boot into the Metropolitan Police in the UK for years now. The Casey Review into the Met (*see also* p. 65) found that senior management took a 'defensive attitude to these scandals – playing them down and dismissing them as procedural issues rather than holding up their hands, listening and seeking to change'.[22]

Indian educational technology company Byju, despite there being a multitude of allegations from staff (including copies of WhatsApp messages and emails and call recordings) of a toxic workplace culture,[23] [24] continue to insist that nothing is wrong.

A spokesperson (more on that shortly) for Byju said that those who speak out represent 'an infinitesimal percentage' of its employees and that they continue to have a 'zero tolerance for unpleasant behaviour in the workplace'.

They also claim to have a world-class HR function.

Gaming company Activision Blizzard have faced many allegations of toxic culture and yet despite the serious nature of some of the reports – people being sacked for reporting their harassers,[25] nursing mothers' breast milk being stolen from fridges[26] and suicide as a result of harassment – CEO Bobby Kotick decided to blame unions instead.

In an interview with *Variety*,[27] Kotick said, 'We did not have a systemic issue with harassment – ever, but what we did have was a very aggressive labour movement working hard to try and destabilize the company.'

Award-winning TV show *The Ellen Show* (*see also* p. 75) faced allegations of toxic culture in 2020. Dozens of employees alleged a culture of microaggressions, abusive behaviour and racism. One former employee said, 'That "be kind" bullshit only happens when the cameras are on.'[28]

Posting on X (formerly Twitter) in 2020, comedian Kevin T. Porter alleged that Ellen DeGeneres was 'notoriously one of the meanest people alive' and started a thread for people to share their stories of working with her, which garnered over 300 replies.[29]

According to DeGeneres, in an interview with the *Hollywood Reporter* in 2020, she was told not to address the allegations and said that at the time she felt like, 'I don't deserve this. I don't need this. I know who I am. I'm a good person.'[30]

She sent staff a letter[31] – subsequently leaked to the media – in which she sought to apologize for the culture. However, the 'apology' was roundly criticized[32] as she sought to blame others for the toxicity. She said, 'I've not been able to stay on top of everything and relied on others to do their jobs as they knew I'd want them done. Clearly some didn't.' She continued, 'I'm also learning that people who work with me and for me are speaking on my behalf and misrepresenting who I am and that has to stop.'

In her opening monologue of Season 18, DeGeneres apologized once again,[33] albeit slightly awkwardly, taking full responsibility for the culture and the allegations. But she then moved on quickly and started talking about herself and invoked global events (the pandemic, wildfires, racial injustice) as a way of reframing perspective, all of which made the apology sound a little disingenuous.

It didn't need a monologue; it needed a simple human statement to take full responsibility for what people felt when they worked on the show and a dedication to do better. End.

Here are a couple of better ways to do it.

In April 2023 CBI President Brian McBride sent a letter[34] to all staff once the Fox Williams report had been published. Among other things, he said, 'I will tell you that every member of the CBI's leadership team is devastated and appalled by the substance of these allegations.' He continued, 'Our collective failure to completely protect vulnerable employees, to ensure that the alleged incidents could never happen in the first place, and to put in place proper mechanisms to rapidly escalate incidents of this nature to the level of senior leadership.'

The Whyte Review[35] into the alleged toxicity at British Gymnastics was released in 2022. It blasted the 'unacceptable culture' and found that the organization – and its HR department – kept no records of complaints made by gymnasts for eight years. Anne Whyte KC further described a 'culture of fear' where gymnasts were simply too scared to come forward and report the sexual harassment and abusive behaviour that they endured.[36]

When the report was published, the former British Gymnastics CEO Jane Allen, who had initially indicated that the negative press were to blame, made a full apology, saying, 'I'm deeply sorry I didn't do more for everyone – especially the athletes – to feel supported, able to speak up and be heard. There's nothing more vital. This was under my leadership and it should have been different.'[37]

While apologies will never be able to reverse the treatment that people – and in this case, children – face, they can at least help with the healing process.

When I was in Melbourne, Australia in August 2023, I spoke to crisis communications expert Alex Cramb[38] to better understand how organizations should respond to allegations of toxic culture. Cramb started his working life as a journalist and has worked extensively in the public and private sectors, including as senior press secretary to Anthony Albanese, as part of the team that got him elected as Australian Prime Minister.

Among other things, he now works with organizations to help them address issues of toxic culture and I asked him how organizations should respond when culture makes it to the media. Cramb said, 'It starts with figuring out whether there's a willingness from the executive to actually deal with toxic culture. In my experience, toxic culture can often be encouraged or incentivized in order to achieve targets, so some leaders don't want to accept they've been complicit.'

I often hear this referred to as 'hustle culture', yet I know and have worked with many teams that have targets to hit, and who manage to do so, thanks to the vibrant culture they've created.

Cramb continued, 'In many cases, organizations underestimate the damage to the brand and reputation that this kind of story can have. They'll try and pass it off with statements such as "it's only a few people" in the hope that it will go away. However, a good journalist will always know where to look.'

We talked about a couple of case studies where organizations have tried to use legal language as a way of trying to confuse people as to what the real issues are. Cramb felt that this strategy doesn't work as culture is now a story that people are interested in: 'The media will keep driving the story these days to get to the ethical, moral and, ultimately, human angle.' I asked him to provide some insights into the steps that he advises his clients to take when they find themselves in the media. He suggests the following approach:

1. Tell the truth and be as transparent as possible – don't lie, cover up or use legalese to try and confuse people.

2. Lean into the problem – be prepared to hear things you don't know or understand and figure out what's been done, what should have been done and what's yet to be done.

3. Move quickly – if a review is required, seek outside help and get it underway as soon as possible. Keep communicating the timeline internally throughout this process.

4. Apologize – should the review confirm the allegations as made, then a full and frank apology is required. Don't try and sell the positives, talk about the action that will be taken to remedy the situation.

5. Provide a timetable – and provide reports/press releases on the actions being taken, ensuring that they're not Band-Aids to cover a gaping wound.

Despite taking this approach, Cramb says that senior leaders should still expect bad press, but 'it's not the initial transgression that will keep them reporting on you, it'll be about how they move forward that counts.'

Finally, I asked him about one of my pet hates. For me, there's no worse response to toxic culture than sending a 'spokesperson' out to do a senior leader's job. A spokesperson is often used when an organization doesn't wish to admit culpability for something that has not yet been proven, yet what it really demonstrates is that senior leaders understand that their reputations are on the line and they're not prepared to risk them until a report is finalized and they have someone or something else to complain about.

Fair enough – you might think – but imagine how it looks to the rest of the world, when no one can be bothered to take responsibility, publicly, for the allegations being made. I asked Cramb whether he'd agree with this.

'One hundred per cent,' he told me. 'It's entirely the role of a CEO or senior leading partner to front-foot these issues and be prepared to answer questions candidly and to the best of their ability. Otherwise, the media will keep hounding them until they do.'

When the CEO is front and centre answering questions, it demonstrates ownership and commitment to do things in the correct way and is also an illustration to employees (current and future) that culture – and the treatment of humans within it – is something that the organization takes seriously.

Not all toxic cultures are made equally

That said, not every report will establish that there is a toxic culture. As I said at the start of this book, just because someone alleges that it is, doesn't make it so. Indeed, organizations are increasingly fighting back against those that seek to deliberately harm the reputation of others through scurrilous allegations.

Also, while in Melbourne, I spoke to Paul O'Halloran, Partner at law firm Dentons. I had a fascinating meeting with him, listening to stories where organizations have been successful in challenging bullying claims through the courts.

It's important to state here that I'm not advocating that organizations act defensively upon claims of toxicity being made and then seek to bully those that make them through the threat of legal action. However, there also needs to be an acceptance that there are some people in the world – often with unsatisfied professional expectations – that make malicious claims and this needs to be established *before* an investigation is initiated.

For the most part, organizations will seek to avoid the media spotlight and reach a financial settlement with those making the allegations, regardless of whether they are true or not. Yet according to O'Halloran, more and more organizations are now pushing back on scurrilous claims in order to maintain the reputation – and the vibrancy – of their culture. In these instances, Paul said that it's important that organizations carefully assess the situation before commissioning a review. He gave me some good examples of employees being performance managed by their organization, who then claim that they're being bullied, when in reality, 'they are constantly disobedient in the face of lawful and obedient directions'. He added that it's really important that organizations treat this as a disciplinary action taken against an individual, rather than 'destroy the fabric of the workplace by bringing in an investigator who interviews 45 people and introduces turbulence, stemming from one person's overly subjective views about their treatment'.

Paul presented me with some interesting case studies from the Fair Work Commission[39] in Australia. Each country will have its own legislation that protects employees and employers alike and it's up to the courts (if it makes it that far) to determine how the law should be interpreted. Two in particular caught my attention. In the case Kordek vs Marsh Pty Ltd (FWC Case 6972 – 2020), the commission stated, 'the vast majority of stop bullying applications are brought by persons who are the subject of disciplinary or performance issues and the application used to deflect attention from their own shortcomings.'

And this one from Tanka Jang Karki (FWC Case 3147 – 2019): 'it is not acceptable to use the stop bullying jurisdiction as a shield or stalking horse, to prevent, delay or deflect justifiable disciplinary outcomes.'

In instances where employees allege bullying, but the employer sees it as performance management, it's important that the employer investigates the bullying claim first before taking any action on the performance. Should they terminate the employment based on performance, the employer then has to disprove that the alleged bullying had anything to do with the termination.

To reiterate, I'm not suggesting here that organizations use the law to intimidate or obfuscate a genuine grievance. However, there are often personalities in the workplace who want unequivocal vindication (not necessarily money) from a third party that they've been wronged, when often their behaviour or performance is the issue.

Organizations should still treat these employees with empathy and compassion, however. Disagreement over the perception of a situation doesn't mean that a lack of humanity can be applied to it. The issue should be dealt with swiftly and decisively, and the organization should learn from it and – at the very least – ensure that the person isn't allowed to return.

Paul O'Halloran told me of one case where an employer paid off an individual that alleged a toxic culture and bullying, only for another department in the organization to hire them back just three months later! The individual made the same claim about the new department, at which point the organization realized the mistake they'd made and terminated the employee's contract.

It cannot be underestimated just how tricky these situations can be. However, leaders need to understand how to navigate these issues well. That is, the determination between dealing with a toxic individual, as opposed to a toxic culture.

Scenario testing can help, as can a well-written risk management plan that can be activated, should toxic culture be alleged. Ultimately, if the allegations are serious and/or multitudinous, senior leaders need to move quickly to investigate and independence is critically important. As you will have seen throughout this book, most – if not all – of the most serious allegations have been investigated by barristers or lawyers. This not only provides integrity, but also ensures that the organization doesn't 'mark its own homework' (i.e. tells itself that it's right) or that the claims aren't buried or whitewashed. They keep to the timescales they've been given and interview people without prejudice or bias. In short, they are focused on the facts and the facts alone.

They recognize that taking too long to complete the review will adversely affect the prevailing culture and leaders who invest in independent investigation can be assured that no stone will be left unturned as to the root cause of the issues and the actions required to address them.

Detox your culture: actions

In my experience, how an organization chooses to respond to toxic culture allegations is often the difference between how their employees and the general public view the leadership team.

The Spanish Football Association brought shame on themselves and Spain as a country with the way that they dealt with the Rubiales case. That it was ever allowed to get to this point is an utter failure of leadership.

It's not enough to hope that you're never faced with allegations of toxic culture, it's a risk that needs to be continually assessed and mitigated so that if it should eventualize, the organization understands the action that needs to be taken. And if an apology is required then it should be genuine, demonstrate your understanding of the situation, focused on the victims, and contain a list of the actions that will be undertaken to affect the change required. After all, apologies without changes will just be seen as manipulation and that will elicit another response that may worsen the situation further.

Five things:

1. Build a culture where it's safe for staff to speak up.
2. Ensure that pulse surveys are undertaken regularly.
3. If feedback is provided, action must be taken to address it.
4. Seek independent help, should the allegations warrant it.
5. Apologize unreservedly and provide updates on the actions being taken.

CHAPTER ELEVEN

What to do if you work in a toxic culture now

'No person – in whatever job, in whatever industry – should have to forfeit professional aspirations and the right to earn a living to the abusive whims of the powerful.'

Ashley Judd lawsuit against Harvey Weinstein[1]

If you find yourself in a workplace with a terrible culture, then it's important that you think carefully about your next move. If you don't believe the situation will improve then looking for another job has to be a priority for the sake of your mental and physical health. In your exit interview – assuming one exists – you can outline the reasons for your departure in order to help others in a similar position.

If, however, leaving is not an option for you, it's important to approach the situation thoughtfully and ethically, particularly if you're thinking of making allegations via social media. Here are some steps to consider:

Document the Issues: Before taking any action, gather evidence and documentation of what you consider to be problematic practices. These could include emails, messages, photos or any other relevant material that highlights the issues you want to address. Any kind of recordings require consent and may breach privacy laws so that needs to be taken into consideration.

Understand the Consequences: Exposing workplace practices can have both positive and negative consequences. While it might bring attention to the issues, it could also result in legal action, or even damage to your own professional reputation. Reporting inappropriate cultural practices or behaviours should never produce negative consequences for the person reporting them. However, in toxic cultures anything is possible.

Internal Channels: If you feel able to approach your manager or HR department (if your manager is the problem) to talk about the issues in confidence then that's what you should do. Depending on the action they take, there may not be a need to make the issue public.

Anonymity: If your organization employs a whistle-blowing approach to feedback, then this could be a way for you to lessen the risk of any consequences you feel may come your way. If you decide to use social media, think about whether you want to reveal your identity. Depending on the severity of the issues, you might want to consider posting anonymously to protect yourself from potential repercussions.

Choose the Right Platform: Choose a social media platform that is appropriate for the message you want to convey. Platforms like Twitter, LinkedIn or even Glassdoor might be suitable for professional concerns, while Instagram or TikTok might be more visual and engaging.

Craft a Thoughtful Message: Be clear, concise and objective in your messaging. Stick to facts and avoid personal attacks. Focus on the issues at hand rather than venting frustration.

Protect Sensitive Information: Avoid sharing sensitive or confidential information that could harm individuals or the company itself. Stick to general practices and behaviours that are causing problems, rather than naming specific individuals.

Offer Solutions: Alongside highlighting the issues, propose potential solutions to the problems you're addressing (provided they're not purely behaviour related). This shows that you're not just complaining, but genuinely interested in making positive changes.

Prepare for Backlash: Be prepared for potential backlash, both from your employer and the public. Make sure you are mentally and emotionally prepared for any negative responses that may come your way.

Legal Implications: Understand the legal implications of your actions. Depending on your jurisdiction and the nature of your actions, you could be subject to defamation or other legal actions.

Seek External Advice: Consider seeking advice from legal professionals, your union representative (if you have one), colleagues, friends, or family members before taking any action. They can offer different perspectives and insights that might help you make an informed decision.

Monitor and Engage Responsibly: If you do decide to expose workplace practices on social media, be prepared to engage responsibly with the discussions that arise. Be open to constructive criticism and avoid escalating conflicts.

Remember that the decision to expose workplace practices is not without its risks. It should always be dealt with internally to begin with and if you don't feel like your concerns are being addressed then you need to think carefully about your next steps.

It will come as no surprise to you that I recommend that you leave any organization that doesn't treat its people with respect. However, as a realist, I understand that this is not always possible to do. If you feel that you're being physically threatened or harassed, then you should gather your evidence and consider reporting the incident to the authorities. It's a sad fact that many people still face varying levels of sexual harassment and assault in the workplace, so if it feels safe for you to speak up, either internally or externally, then it can help. That said, anyone who notices any kind of inappropriate behaviour directed at an individual or group of individuals should also speak up. Too many cultures have turned toxic because people have turned a blind eye to what they've seen: don't be that person.

Anxiety, stress, depression and suicidal thoughts are all hallmarks of toxic cultures too. Help and support is available to you through organizations such as The Samaritans in the UK (www.samaritans.org) and US (www.samaritansusa.org), AASRA in India (www.aasra.info) or Beyond Blue in Australia (www.beyondblue.com.au) to name a few. You are not alone.

Conclusion

Toxic culture is not inevitable. It's easy to think that having read this book. However, it's not – there are more stagnant, pleasant, combatant and vibrant cultures than there are toxic ones. Indeed, I always feel a great sadness when I read or hear about toxic culture and the instances of it in the media are increasing. That's partly a result of the fact that we're now taking the mental health and unjust treatment of employees more seriously – and that's a good thing. Partly, it's a result of media negativity bias. After all, there are lots of fabulous working cultures, but how many of those do you get to read about?

Actually, if we had more of the latter, then maybe some of the former would use them as inspiration to address their own cultures. Sometimes all people need are some practical stories of things that others do well to help them with their own issues. As I've discussed at length in this book there are many steps you can take to detox your culture and dramatically reduce the risk of losing good people, missing targets or appearing in the news. But you have to *want* to spend money and time to do this, not talk about it in the hope that it sorts itself out.

The root causes of most – if not all – of the case studies in this book are:

1. A lack of understanding – of the importance of culture, the pillars of it and the structures required to build and maintain it.
2. A lack of investment – in the activities required to bring people together and give them the opportunity to define and evolve what the culture needs to be.
3. Poor leadership – from those that understand both points 1 and 2 and choose to ignore it, putting profit or pandering to a higher body before people.

Once the source of the toxicity has been addressed, the culture will improve but only if positive action is continually taken to inject new ideas, energy and a different perspective to create a new foundation for employees moving forward. Like I said, toxic culture isn't an inevitability but without taking steps to detox your culture, it most definitely will be.

Let the detox begin!

Colin D. Ellis

About the Author

Colin D. Ellis is a four-time bestselling author, an award-winning international public speaker and a highly sought-after Culture Consultant. He has worked with almost 100 different cultures in a multitude of sectors in 15 countries (and counting!) around the world. His clients include companies such as Red Bull, Cisco, Manulife Insurance, ANZ Bank, VMware, KPMG, US House of Representatives and many others looking to make a difference to the way that work gets done.

Originally from Liverpool in the UK, he spent six years working in New Zealand before moving to Australia with his wife and two children. In between work assignments, he now splits his time between Europe and Australia in the hope that the kids can't find him!

When he is not speaking or writing, Colin likes to watch his favourite sports teams in action – Everton in the English Premier League and the Los Angeles Dodgers US baseball team. Although the latter definitely gives him more pleasure (currently!) than the former.

You can find out more about Colin, contact him with work enquiries, listen to his podcasts or follow him on social media via any of the links below:

Personal

Website: www.colindellis.com
Newsletter: www.colindellis.com/boom
Contact: hello@colindellis.com

Social

LinkedIn: www.linkedin.com/in/colindellis
YouTube: www.youtube.com/colindellis
Instagram: www.instagram.com/colindellis

Podcasts

Culture & Coffee: podcasters.spotify.com/pod/cultureandcoffee
Inside Out Culture: insideoutculture.buzzsprout.com

Music List

For those who have read any of my previous books, you'll know that often this section is actually the most popular! I even had one person tell me that it's the section that they always read first. People like to pick apart my state of mind through the music that I listen to while I'm writing and some even like to accost me at conferences for daring to listen to 'music that betrays your northern England, indie-loving roots' (you know who you are!).

I need music when I'm writing because silence saps my energy. Songs with words are fine while I'm researching and capturing ideas. However, I move to instrumentals/classical music when I'm actually writing to avoid the distraction that singing induces so it's only right that I credit the people who helped me to write this book without giving them any money, obviously. So, here's this book's playlist. I've reconnected with some of my old favourites and indulged in some new stuff too. I also owe a debt of thanks to the late, great UK DJ Stu Allan, whose *Old Skool Nation* mixes kept my energy up during the research phase.

These were the artists and albums that helped me through the writing process:

808:88:98 – *808 State*
Air – *Moon Safari*
Alvvays – *Blue Rev*
Arctic Monkeys – *The Car*
The Beatles – *Help!*
Boards of Canada – *Tomorrow's Harvest*
Brian Eno – *Ambient 1: Music for Airports*

Brian Eno – *Ambient 4: On Land*

The City of Prague Orchestra – *The Film Music of John Williams*

Derek B – *Bullet from a Gun*

Dionne Warwick – *I'll Never Love This Way Again*

Doves – *Lost Souls*

Doves – *The Last Broadcast*

Editors – *EBM*

The Farm – *Pastures Old and New*

Fred Again... & Brian Eno – *Secret Life*

Haircut 100 – *Pelican West*

Harry Styles – *Harry's House*

Ian Brown – *Ripples*

John Williams – *Greatest Hits 1969–1999*

Kraftwerk – *Trans-Europe Express*

London Grammar – *Californian Soil*

London Grammar – *The Remixes*

The National – *First Two Pages of Frankenstein*

Noel Gallagher's High Flying Birds – *Back the Way We Came: Vol. 1*

Noel Gallagher's High Flying Birds – *Council Skies*

Paul Weller – *Paul Weller*

The Police – *Reggatta de Blanc*

Public Service Broadcasting – *Every Valley*

Public Service Broadcasting – *The Race for Space*

Radiohead – *Amnesiac*

Radiohead – *Kid A*

Rival Consoles – *Now Is*

The Smiths – *Strangeways Here We Come*

The Smiths – *The Queen is Dead*

The Stone Roses – *The Stone Roses*

Suede – *Dog Man Star*

Suede – *Sci-Fi and Lullabies*

Suede – *Suede*
Sufjan Stevens – *Come on! Feel the Illinoise!*
The Tea Street Band – *Frequency*
The Tea Street Band – *Tea Street Band*
Trashcan Sinatras – *Cake*
Troye Sivan – *Bloom*

IS YOUR CULTURE TOXIC?

Take the Culture Quiz and find out!

www.colindellis.com/culture-quiz

Take a short, easy quiz for
a free culture report

Acknowledgements

Huge thanks to the team at Bloomsbury – Ian, Allie, Aimee and to Jane for all their work in not only getting the book ready for publication, but also for their management of this project and their timely challenges to my content and thinking.

Thanks to my clients, for putting their faith in me to help them to create great places to work. The work that you do on a day-to-day basis to build a great culture and experience for your people, continues to be a source of inspiration to me.

To my closest friends – specifically Simon, Digby, Monique and Sophie – thank you for being there when I needed you most. Writing a book can often be a frustrating business, so our regular calls, catch ups and (of course) karaoke sessions are things that I continue to look forward to.

And to my family, without whose love, trust, patience and understanding it would be impossible for me to do the work that I love doing. There should be way more guilt-tripping and piss-taking of my stories than there currently is, and for that I'll always be grateful.

References

Epigraph

1   https://open.spotify.com/show/0Z0KhuivFm1Ry4WIpWspPv

Introduction

1   https://pmq.shrm.org/wp-content/uploads/2020/07/SHRM-Culture
     -Report_2019-1.pdf
2   https://www.ft.com/content/59211933-5494-4b35-b3e5-a0a791b1fd18
3   https://sloanreview.mit.edu/article/why-every-leader-needs-to-worry-
     about-toxic-culture/
4   https://www.bloomberg.com/news/articles/2022-01-11/what-s-driving
     -the-great-resignation-toxic-culture-is-a-bigger-driver-than-pay
5   https://sloanreview.mit.edu/article/how-to-fix-a-toxic-culture/
6   https://pmq.shrm.org/wp-content/uploads/2020/07/SHRM-Culture
     -Report_2019-1.pdf
7   https://www.parliament.nz/en/visit-and-learn/how-parliament
     -works/office-of-the-speaker/corporate-documents/independent
     -external-review-into-bullying-and-harassment-in-the-new-zealand
     -parliamentary-workplace-final-report/
8   https://sloanreview.mit.edu/article/why-every-leader-needs-to-worry
     -about-toxic-culture/
9   https://www.forbes.com/sites/josiecox/2023/03/14/new-research
     -reveals-workplace-toxic-culture-gap-between-women-and-men
     /https://www.forbes.com/sites/josiecox/2023/03/14/new-research
     -reveals-workplace-toxic-culture-gap-between-women-and-men/
10   https://www.parliament.nz/en/visit-and-learn/how-parliament
     -works/office-of-the-speaker/corporate-documents/independent
     -external-review-into-bullying-and-harassment-in-the-new-zealand
     -parliamentary-workplace-final-report/
11   https://sloanreview.mit.edu/article/why-every-leader-needs-to-worry
     -about-toxic-culture/

12 https://www.nzherald.co.nz/nz/housing-new-zealand-workers
-suspected-suicide-after-alleged-bullying-not-notified-to-worksafe-for
-six-months/H33UJUG4EVYAVBIMB524L265LA/?c_id=1&objectid
=12040773

13 https://sloanreview.mit.edu/article/how-to-fix-a-toxic-culture/

Chapter 1: What is toxic culture?

1 https://metro.co.uk/2023/06/11/dancing-on-ice-star-jason-gardiner
-hits-out-at-itvs-toxic-culture-18931332/

2 https://www.manchestereveningnews.co.uk/news/tv/phillip-schofield
-releases-new-statement-27013029

3 https://news.sky.com/story/holly-willoughby-says-phillip-schofield
-lied-to-her-about-affair-in-first-statement-since-relationship-emerged
-12891187

4 https://www.standard.co.uk/showbiz/who-martin-frizell-phillip
-schofield-this-morning-b1084700.html

5 https://news.sky.com/story/this-morning-key-extracts-from-itv-chief
-executives-letter-to-culture-secretary-on-phillip-schofield-departure
-12893853

6 https://www.youtube.com/watch?v=rWvpvlT9pJU

7 https://www.washingtonpost.com/world/2021/11/20/colombia-police
-nazi-germany-president/

8 https://www.colombiaemb.org/post/president-duque-announces
-reforms-to-comprehensively-transform-colombian-police-force

9 https://globalnews.ca/news/9771094/upei-workplace-misconduct
-allegation-review/

10 https://www.cbsnews.com/news/fixing-a-toxic-culture-like-ubers
-requires-more-than-just-a-new-ceo/

11 https://www.kcur.org/news/2022-09-15/hundreds-of-amazon-workers
-in-missouri-speak-out-for-better-pay-and-conditions-we-were-unsafe

12 https://dotesports.com/news/ubisoft-employees-blame-the-companys
-toxic-culture-for-continued-issues

13 https://www.opindia.com/2022/09/ex-buzzfeed-employees-talk-about
-toxic-work-culture-try-guys-ned-fulmer-infidelity/

14 https://www.theglobeandmail.com/sports/olympics/article-report
-reveals-toxic-culture-within-rowing-canadas-high-performance/

15 https://www.abc.net.au/radio/programs/am/toxic-culture-at-australia-s
-antarctic-base-exposed/14064324

16 https://www.theverge.com/2023/6/1/23744109/activision-blizzard
-bobby-kotick-denies-harassment-variety

17 https://edition.cnn.com/2020/07/31/entertainment/ellen-degeneres
-apology-email/index.html/

18 https://www.telegraph.co.uk/women/life/world-cup-kiss-anti-feminism
-spain-luis-rubiales/

19 https://www.forbes.com/sites/jackkelly/2021/01/12/chinas-toxic-work
-culture-results-in-deaths-and-suicide/

20 https://www.nzherald.co.nz/nz/housing-new-zealand-workers
-suspected-suicide-after-alleged-bullying-not-notified-to-worksafe-for
-six-months/H33UJUG4EVYAVBIMB524L265LA/

21 https://sloanreview.mit.edu/article/how-to-fix-a-toxic-culture/

22 https://futureforum.com/pulse-survey/

23 https://www.shrm.org/hr-today/news/hr-magazine/winter2019/pages/
workplace-culture-matters.aspx

24 https://www.bloomberg.com/news/articles/2022-01-11/what-s-driving
-the-great-resignation-toxic-culture-is-a-bigger-driver-than-pay

25 https://inews.co.uk/sport/football/everton-fans-moshiri-board
-everything-wrong-club-2083064

26 https://sloanreview.mit.edu/article/why-every-leader-needs-to-worry
-about-toxic-culture

27 https://www.gallup.com/workplace/349484/state-of-the-global
-workplace-2022-report.aspx

28 https://www.psychologytoday.com/us/blog/conscious-communication
/201803/why-work-stress-is-bad-for-your-relationships

29 https://www2.deloitte.com/content/dam/Deloitte/at/Documents/
human-capital/at-is-your-organization-simply-irresistible.pdf

30 https://www.gettysburg.edu/news/stories?id=79db7b34-630c-4f49
-ad32-4ab9ea48e72b

31 https://www.hhs.gov/sites/default/files/workplace-mental-health-well
-being.pdf

32 https://www.gartner.com/en/newsroom/press-releases/2017-10-02
-gartner-survey-of-more-than-3000-cios-confirms-the-changing-role
-of-the-chief-information-officer

33 https://www.jstor.org/stable/e26610964

34 https://assets.publishing.service.gov.uk/government/uploads/system/
uploads/attachment_data/file/610130/Duty_of_Care_Review_-_April
_2017__2.pdf

35 https://www.gallup.com/workplace/238085/state-american-workplace
-report-2017.aspx

36 https://fortune.com/ranking/best-companies/

37 https://bit.ly/3CKu7o5

38 https://www.limeade.com/wp-content/uploads/2019/09/
LimeadeInstitute_TheScienceOfCare_Whitepaper_Web.pdf

39 https://www.birminghammail.co.uk/news/local-news/short---campbell
-is-a-bully-42739

40 https://en.wikipedia.org/wiki/Malcolm_Tucker

41 https://en.wikipedia.org/wiki/The_Thick_of_It

42 https://www.radiotimes.com/tv/comedy/armando-iannucci-malcolm
-tucker-exclusive-newsupdate/

43 https://nypost.com/2023/06/21/credit-suisse-investors-sue-over-toxic
-culture-at-nyc-office/

44 https://www.britannica.com/event/Jonestown

45 https://www.primevideo.com/detail/WeWork-Or-the-Making-and
-Breaking-of-a-47-Billion-Unicorn/0GQLZRMTZ8JHXNW0MMP
62PQUB0

46 https://www.theguardian.com/business/2023/nov/06/wework
-bankruptcy-debt-remote-work

47 https://www.amazon.com/Corporate-Cults-Insidious-All-Consuming
-Organization/dp/0814404936

Chapter 2: What's the plan?

1 https://downloads.ctfassets.net/8aefmxkxpxwl/3d835a7MATY05Yv
lprREg9/cba93c9257e4d26e28e266d3d260fab1/UBI2021_URD_EN
_COMPLET_Vmel_160621.pdf?stream=top

2 https://www.letelegramme.fr/economie/toute-l-actualite/ubisoft-peine
   -a-tourner-la-page-dun-management-toxique-3787085.php

3 https://www.gamesindustry.biz/report-details-toxic-culture-sexual
   -harassment-and-racial-pay-disparity-at-ubisoft-singapore

4 https://www.gamesindustry.biz/ubisoft-has-reportedly-made-minimal
   -changes-following-abuse-allegations

5 https://downloads.ctfassets.net/8aefmxkxpxwl/3d835a7MATY05Yv
   lprREg9/cba93c9257e4d26e28e266d3d260fab1/UBI2021_URD_EN
   _COMPLET_Vmel_160621.pdf?stream=top

6 https://www.thenationalnews.com/business/nissan-says-carlos-ghosn
   -was-deified-in-toxic-corporate-culture-1.842453

7 https://global.nissannews.com/en/releases/230511-01-e#

8 https://www.glassdoor.com/Overview/Working-at-Nissan-EI_IE3535
   .11,17.htm

9 https://blogs.microsoft.com/blog/2023/01/18/subject-focusing-on-our
   -short-and-long-term-opportunity/

10 https://www.theguardian.com/technology/2023/mar/14/mark
   -zuckerberg-meta-layoffs-hiring-freeze

11 https://www.washingtonpost.com/technology/2023/06/09/meta-morale
   -artificial-intelligence/

12 https://about.fb.com/news/2021/10/founders-letter/

13 https://www.theguardian.com/technology/commentisfree/2023/may
   /13/death-of-mark-zuckerberg-metaverse-meta-facebook-virtual
   -reality-ai

14 https://en.wikipedia.org/wiki/Wells_Fargo_cross-selling_scandal

15 https://www.vanityfair.com/news/2017/05/wells-fargo-corporate
   -culture-fraud

16 https://www.forbes.com/sites/halahtouryalai/2012/01/25/the-gospel
   -according-to-wells-fargo/?sh=10b9af4c7904

17 https://www.newyorker.com/business/currency/the-record-fine-against
   -wells-fargo-points-to-the-failure-of-regulation

18 https://www.nytimes.com/2016/10/21/business/dealbook/voices-from
   -wells-fargo-i-thought-i-was-having-a-heart-attack.html?_r=0

19 https://www.npr.org/2016/10/04/496508361/former-wells-fargo
   -employees-describe-toxic-sales-culture-even-at-hq

20 https://www.nytimes.com/2016/10/21/business/dealbook/voices-from
-wells-fargo-i-thought-i-was-having-a-heart-attack.html?_r=0

21 https://www.bloomberg.com/news/articles/2017-04-10/wells-fargo
-rehires-about-1-000-staff-in-wake-of-account-scandal

22 https://www.theguardian.com/business/2019/jan/04/wells-fargo-fake
-accounts-scandal-employees

23 https://www.amazon.com.au/Fit-Disruption-transform-business-thrive
-ebook/dp/B086R8N4LK

24 https://mediaassets.kjrh.com/html/pdfs/unhappyemployees_gallup
.pdf

25 https://www.pwc.com/gx/en/issues/upskilling/global-culture-survey
-2021.html

26 https://www.reuters.com/business/aerospace-defense/southwest
-airlines-operations-back-normal-after-being-crippled-by-storm-2022
-12-30/

27 https://knowledge.wharton.upenn.edu/podcast/knowledge-at-wharton
-podcast/the-demise-of-toys-r-us

28 https://www.usatoday.com/story/money/2018/03/15/toys-r-us
-liquidation-amazon-target-walmart/427209002/

29 https://brand-minds.medium.com/the-downfall-of-toys-r-us-dont
-blame-amazon-c88856516383

Chapter 3: What good are you doing?

1 https://www.fastcompany.com/3041738/millennials-want-to-work-at
-organizations-that-focus-on-purpose-not-just-p

2 https://eric.ed.gov/?id=EJ880363

3 https://www.researchgate.net/publication/5521509_Understanding_the
_Search_for_Meaning_in_Life_Personality_Cognitive_Style_and_the
_Dynamic_Between_Seeking_and_Experiencing_Meaning

4 https://www.researchgate.net/publication/289194122_Work_as_
Meaning_Individual_and_Organizational_Benefits_of_Engaging_in
_Meaningful_Work

5 https://joshbersin.com/wp-content/uploads/2021/12/WT-21_12-HR
-Predictions-for-2022-Report.pdf

6 https://www.herbertsmithfreehills.com/latest-thinking/the-new-world
   -of-work-report-warns-of-an-unprecedented-rise-in-workplace
   -activism-v2

7 https://www.theguardian.com/technology/2018/nov/01/google
   -walkout-global-protests-employees-sexual-harassment-scandals

8 https://www.ecowatch.com/employee-climate-activism-2645855023
   .html

9 https://www.nytimes.com/2021/04/30/technology/basecamp-politics
   -ban-resignations.html

10 https://www.nytimes.com/2021/04/30/technology/basecamp-politics
   -ban-resignations.html

11 https://www.theverge.com/2021/5/4/22419799/basecamp-ceo
   -apologizes-staff-new-post

12 https://www.socialcapitalpartnerships.com/chris-miller

13 https://joshbersin.com/wp-content/uploads/2021/04/Big-Reset
   -Playbook_Whats-Working-Now_Josh-Bersin_2020.pdf

14 https://www.foxbusiness.com/features/what-the-heck-is-a-chief
   -purpose-officer

15 *Virgin by Design* (Thames and Hudson Ltd, 2020) by Nick Carson

16 https://www.johnelkington.com/archive/TBL-elkington-chapter.pdf

17 https://www.techtarget.com/whatis/definition/environmental-social
   -and-governance-ESG

18 https://www.theatlantic.com/business/archive/2015/06/patagonia-labor
   -clothing-factory-exploitation/394658/

19 https://www.outsideonline.com/2155931/outdoor-industry-pushes
   -back-against-utah

20 https://www.greatplacetowork.com/certified-company/1000745

21 https://www.mckinsey.com/business-functions/organization/our
   -insights/purpose-shifting-from-why-to-how

22 https://web.archive.org/web/20140819180035/http://theranos.com/our
   -company

23 https://www.elle.com/culture/movies-tv/a39281820/where-is-elizabeth
   -holmes-now/

24 https://edition.cnn.com/2019/10/25/world/lion-air-crash-report/index
   .html

25 https://www.nytimes.com/2019/12/23/business/Boeing-ceo
    -muilenburg.html
26 https://www.npr.org/2021/08/24/1030787092/regulators-are
    -investigating-boeings-safety-culture-amid-complaints-by-its-engineers
27 https://www.nbcnews.com/news/us-news/faa-investigate-boeing-door
    -plug-falls-alaska-airlines-plane-midair-rcna133491
28 https://www.boeing.com/features/innovation-quarterly/2022/05/the
    -power-of-purpose.page

Chapter 4: Are you set up to succeed?

 1 https://www.met.police.uk/SysSiteAssets/media/downloads/met/about
    -us/baroness-casey-review/update-march-2023/baroness-casey-review
    -march-2023.pdf
 2 https://globalnews.ca/news/9773845/pei-premier-slams-upei
    -harassment-report/
 3 https://www.theguardian.com/business/2023/may/28/ex-this-morning
    -doctor-ranj-singh-says-culture-on-show-became-toxic
 4 https://globalnews.ca/news/9771094/upei-workplace-misconduct
    -allegation-review/
 5 https://www.thestar.com/news/canada/2023/06/22/upei-board-chair
    -resigns-after-report-of-toxic-culture-says-new-leadership-is-needed
    .html
 6 https://www.brianheger.com/the-state-of-organizations-2023-report
    -mckinsey-company/
 7 https://www.cbi.org.uk/media/lkto4nzv/a-renewed-cbi-prospectus.pdf
 8 https://screenrant.com/nintendo-workplace-culture-report-contractors
    -toxic/
 9 https://www.hcamag.com/au/news/general/why-hr-needs-to-get-better
    -at-managing-toxic-employees/410025
10 https://www.met.police.uk/police-forces/metropolitan-police/areas/
    about-us/about-the-met/bcr/baroness-casey-review/
11 https://protect-advice.org.uk/sue-gray-full-report-published-protect
    -statement/
12 https://www.lansingstatejournal.com/story/news/local/2016/12/15/
    michigan-state-sexual-assault-harassment-larry-nassar/94993582/

13   https://www.lansingstatejournal.com/story/news/local/2016/12/15/
michigan-state-sexual-assault-harassment-larry-nassar/94993582/

14   https://www.jstor.org/stable/2090773

15   https://www.amnesty.org/en/documents/org60/9763/2019/en/

16   https://www.theguardian.com/world/2019/feb/06/amnesty
-international-has-toxic-working-culture-report-finds

17   https://www.brianheger.com/the-state-of-organizations-2023-report
-mckinsey-company/

Chapter 5: What do you value?

1   https://www.investopedia.com/updates/enron-scandal-summary/

2   https://www.justice.gov/archive/opa/pr/2006/May/06_crm_328.html

3   https://www.forbes.com/sites/jackkelly/2020/02/24/wells-fargo
-forced-to-pay-3-billion-for-the-banks-fake-account-scandal/
#14e5c85b42d2

4   https://edition.cnn.com/2020/02/21/business/wells-fargo-settlement
-doj-sec/index.html

5   https://www.bbc.com/news/business-34324772

6   https://www.nbcnews.com/business/autos/judge-approves-largest-fine
-u-s-history-volkswagen-n749406

7   https://www.buzzfeednews.com/article/krystieyandoli/ellen-employees
-allege-toxic-workplace-culture

8   https://www.bbc.com/news/entertainment-arts-54235307

9   https://en.wikipedia.org/wiki/George_Floyd_protests

10   https://www.leadershipiq.com/blogs/leadershipiq/why-company-values
-are-falling-short

11   https://hbr.org/2002/07/make-your-values-mean-something

12   https://mitsloan.mit.edu/ideas-made-to-matter/3-common-myths
-about-work-culture

13   https://www.leadershipiq.com/blogs/leadershipiq/35354241-why-new
-hires-fail-emotional-intelligence-vs-skills

14   https://www2.deloitte.com/content/dam/Deloitte/global/Documents/
deloitte-2022-genz-millennial-survey.pdf

15   https://www.linkedin.com/pulse/millennials-75-workforce-2025-ever
-anita-lettink/

16 https://www2.deloitte.com/content/dam/Deloitte/global/Documents/deloitte-2022-genz-millennial-survey.pdf

17 https://www.theguardian.com/society/2023/jun/21/uks-best-known-retailers-top-list-of-firms-fined-7m-over-pay-breaches

18 https://corporate.marksandspencer.com/sites/marksandspencer/files/2023-06/M per cent26S_2023_Annual_Report.pdf

19 https://papers.ssrn.com/sol3/papers.cfm?abstract_id=2842823

20 https://www.cultureamp.com/resources/homepage-stream/2022-workplace-dei-report?_gl=1*11khpwq*_up*MQ

21 https://www.octanner.com/au/global-culture-report.html

22 https://www.theguardian.com/us-news/2022/may/11/artitifical-intelligence-job-applications-screen-robot-recruiters

23 https://www.brookings.edu/articles/auditing-employment-algorithms-for-discrimination/

24 https://www.rnz.co.nz/news/national/418055/employee-surveillance-software-sales-surge-in-lockdown

25 https://www.vice.com/en/article/88gqgp/mouse-mover-jiggler-app-keep-screen-on-active

26 https://www.whitehouse.gov/ostp/news-updates/2023/05/01/hearing-from-the-american-people-how-are-automated-tools-being-used-to-surveil-monitor-and-manage-workers/

27 https://www.nytimes.com/2022/08/24/podcasts/the-daily/workplace-surveillance-productivity-tracking.html

28 https://www.microsoft.com/en-us/worklab/work-trend-index/hybrid-work-is-just-work

29 https://morningconsult.com/2022/05/31/tech-workers-survey-surveillance/

30 https://www.zappos.com/c/about

31 https://www.amazon.com/Delivering-Happiness-Profits-Passion-Purpose-ebook/dp/B003JTHXN6

32 https://about.google/philosophy/

33 https://www.theguardian.com/australia-news/2022/oct/20/bom-staff-allege-rebranding-debacle-made-toxic-work-culture-even-worse

34 https://www.fastcompany.com/1679907/red-bull-ceo-dietrich-mateschitz-on-brand-as-media-company

Chapter 6: Do managers get it?

1 https://www.rollingstone.com/tv-movies/tv-movie-news/kelly-clarkson
-addresses-toxic-culture-claims-talk-show-investigation-1234734894/
2 https://www.bbc.com/sport/football/35677681
3 https://www.eurosport.com/football/farhad-moshiri-makes-promise-to
-everton-fans_sto5317790/story.shtml
4 https://www.bbc.com/sport/av/football/64309115
5 https://www.mirror.co.uk/sport/football/news/everton-legend
-struggling-come-terms-29014028
6 https://www.liverpoolecho.co.uk/sport/football/football-news/everton
-protests-unfold-inside-outside-25980383
7 https://www.mirror.co.uk/sport/football/news/breaking-everton-ceo
-headlock-safety-28953677
8 https://www.goodisonnews.com/2023/01/18/everton-shareholders
-association-call-for-vote-of-no-confidence-in-clubs-board-of
-directors/
9 https://www.liverpoolecho.co.uk/sport/football/football-news/farhad
-moshiri-everton-interview-breaking-25957342
10 https://www.susanjfowler.com/blog/2017/2/19/reflecting-on-one-very
-strange-year-at-uber
11 https://www.nytimes.com/2017/03/03/technology/uber-greyball
-program-evade-authorities.html
12 https://www.youtube.com/watch?v=NRnq09YRqh8
13 https://www.nytimes.com/2017/06/21/technology/uber-ceo-travis
-kalanick.html
14 https://www.vox.com/2017/6/1/15726882/uber-travis-kalanick-mother
-father-boat-accident
15 https://gizmodo.com/exclusive-the-letter-travis-kalanick-never-sent
-1837881128
16 https://www.theguardian.com/culture/2021/jun/21/sony-music
-australia-allegations-toxic-work-culture
17 https://themusicnetwork.com/sony-music-australia-review-execs-exit/
18 https://www.abc.net.au/news/2021-10-15/ex-sony-boss-denis-handlin
-stripped-of-aria-award/100542820

19   https://www.themandarin.com.au/177821-almost-a-third-of-workers
      -dont-like-their-managers-new-survey-finds/
20   https://news.sky.com/story/hundreds-of-officers-still-in-metropolitan
      -police-should-have-been-sacked-commissioner-sir-mark-rowley-says
      -12959174
21   https://www.pwc.com/gx/en/issues/upskilling/global-culture-survey
      -2021.html
22   https://www.thestar.com.my/sport/swimming/2023/05/24/ex-olympian
      -tells-of-toxic-culture-in-malaysian-swimming
23   https://www.theglobeandmail.com/sports/olympics/article-report
      -reveals-toxic-culture-within-rowing-canadas-high-performance/
24   https://www.theguardian.com/sport/2022/jun/16/british-gymnastics
      -report-anne-whyte-review-uk-sport-gymnasts-abused
25   https://www.theguardian.com/sport/2022/mar/28/canadian-gymnasts
      -call-for-investigation-into-sports-toxic-culture
26   https://bleacherreport.com/articles/2790487-toxic-culture-verbal
      -abuse-outlined-in-espn-report-about-maryland-football-team
27   https://www.slideshare.net/reed2001/culture-1798664#24
28   https://www.espn.com/soccer/story/_/id/37684004/pep-guardiola
      -laughs-row-kevin-de-bruyne-energy
29   https://www.mindtools.com/pages/article/newTED_91.htm
30   https://quoteinvestigator.com/2014/04/06/they-feel/

Chapter 7: Does empathy exist?

1   https://www.punkswithpurpose.org/dearbrewdog/
2   https://www.newsweek.com/americas-most-loved-workplaces-2021
3   https://www.psychologytoday.com/us/therapy-types/emotionally
     -focused-therapy
4   https://www.psychologytoday.com/us/basics/attachment
5   https://www.psychologytoday.com/us/blog/i-hear-you/202001/what
     -does-it-mean-have-insecure-attachment-style
6   https://www.octanner.com/au/global-culture-report.html
7   https://www.hrreporter.com/focus-areas/culture-and-engagement
     /radio-personality-claims-toxic-culture-at-former-employment
     /366903

8   https://www.cbc.ca/news/entertainment/john-derringer-leaves-q107-1
    .6545790

9   https://twitter.com/JennValentyne/status/1529405446393585664

10 https://www.psychologytoday.com/us/blog/hot-thought/201509/
    emotional-capital

11 https://www.amazon.com/Insight-Self-Aware-Ourselves-Clearly
    -Succeed-ebook/dp/B01JWDWP4Y

12 https://www.manageris.com/article-a-better-return-on-self-awareness
    -23932.html

13 https://www.nytimes.com/2021/02/18/business/media/pj-vogt-reply-all
    .html

14 https://hbr.org/2018/01/what-self-awareness-really-is-and-how-to
    -cultivate-it

15 https://www.wsj.com/articles/are-workplace-personality-tests-fair
    -1412044257

16 https://store.hbr.org/product/the-new-rules-of-managing-talent-hbr
    -special-issue/SPFA21

17 https://store.hbr.org/product/the-new-rules-of-managing-talent-hbr
    -special-issue/SPFA21

18 https://drive.google.com/file/d/1WAuyF96HSlj-O0QIbpfHk
    _3MVLqLR0s4/view

19 https://mms.businesswire.com/media/20201007005330/en/828185/1
    /4275411cReworking_Work_Atlassian_and_PaperGiant_en.pdf

20 https://www.businessolver.com/workplace-empathy-executive-summary

21 https://eu.azcentral.com/story/news/local/scottsdale/2022/04/08/
    fired-starbucks-employee-says-management-retaliated-union-effort
    /9507511002/

22 https://perfectunion.us/starbucks-fires-union-leader-laila-dalton/

23 https://www.courthousenews.com/arizona-judge-sides-with-starbucks
    -finding-employee-was-not-fired-for-unionizing/

24 https://www.octanner.com/global-culture-report

25 https://www.octanner.com/au/global-culture-report.html

26 https://www.bloomberg.com/news/articles/2022-01-06/james-hardie
    -fires-ceo-jack-truong-citing-conduct-breaches

27 https://www.reuters.com/business/ousted-james-hardie-ceo-rejects
    -claims-concerns-related-conduct-2022-01-10/

28 https://www.afr.com/companies/manufacturing/ousted-james-hardie
   -boss-rejects-bullying-accusations-20220110-p59n26
29 https://en.wiktionary.org/wiki/camarade
30 https://www.octanner.com/au/global-culture-report.html

Chapter 8: How does work get done?

1 https://edition.cnn.com/2023/05/24/entertainment/melissa-mccarthy
   -work-movies-acting/index.html
2 https://www.researchgate.net/publication/12085280_Building_the_
   Emotional_Intelligence_of_Groups
3 https://www.theguardian.com/tv-and-radio/2015/feb/16/working
   -saturday-night-live-taught-me-ruthlessness-tv
4 https://www.businessinsider.com/saturday-night-live-sexism-horatio
   -sanz-lawsuit-2022-5
5 https://www.who.int/teams/mental-health-and-substance-use/
   promotion-prevention/mental-health-in-the-workplace
6 https://www.instagram.com/p/CRxsq_kBZrP/
7 https://www.huffpost.com/entry/simone-biles-naomi-osaka-mental
   -health-olympics_n_61001bdae4b00fa7af7c385b
8 https://en.wikipedia.org/wiki/Simone_Biles
9 https://edition.cnn.com/politics/live-news/larry-nassar-senate-hearing
   -09-15-21/h_0b79bc8905cc46df9e2f7db83b3a38e9
10 https://edition.cnn.com/2023/08/04/sport/simone-biles-gymnastics
   -return-intl-spt/index.html
11 https://edition.cnn.com/2023/08/04/sport/simone-biles-gymnastics
   -return-intl-spt/index.html
12 https://reimaginaire.medium.com/a-conversation-with-amy
   -edmondson-about-psychological-safety-and-the-future-of-work
   -a0891e137218
13 https://digiday.com/marketing/how-g-fuels-toxic-working
   -environment-made-the-energy-drink-brands-influencer-marketers
   -jump-ship/
14 https://www.canberratimes.com.au/story/6774627/its-like-lord-of-the
   -flies-airservices-australia-review-shows-bullying-sexual-harassment/

15 https://www.jsonline.com/story/communities/lake-country/2023/02 /21/sexual-harassment-common-in-fire-departments-local-research -shows/69925645007/

16 https://www.reuters.com/article/india-education-tech-workers -idINL8N30Z4CC

17 https://www.gallup.com/workplace/349484/state-of-the-global -workplace-2022-report.aspx

18 https://www.perthnow.com.au/politics/nsw-parliament-work-culture -under-scrutiny-c-7846101

19 https://www.ruok.org.au/

20 https://www.dailymail.co.uk/news/article-12342895/Aishwarya -Venkatachalam-Ey-Ernst-Young-Sydney-HQ-David-Larocca -Elizabeth-Broderick.html

21 https://futureforum.com/research/future-forum-pulse-summer -snapshot/

22 https://harrypotter.fandom.com/wiki/Horcrux

23 https://www.forbes.com/sites/edwardsegal/2021/02/17/leaders-and -employees-are-burning-out-at-record-rates-new-survey/

24 https://www.ft.com/content/59211933-5494-4b35-b3e5-a0a791b1fd18

25 https://www.scirp.org/journal/paperinformation.aspx?paperid=75256

26 https://reclaim.ai/blog/task-management-trends-report

27 https://www.limeade.com/wp-content/uploads/2019/09/ LimeadeInstitute_TheScienceOfCare_Whitepaper_Web.pdf

28 https://www.businessinsider.com.au/shopify-ceo-success-long-hours -40-hour-week-2019-12?r=US&IR=T

29 https://en.wikipedia.org/wiki/El_Khomri_law

30 https://smu.emeritus.org/digital-transformation

31 https://qatalog.com/blog/post/work-isnt-working-press-release/

32 https://www.theguardian.com/technology/2023/jan/20/davos-elite-say -gen-z-workers-prefer-chat-to-email

33 https://www.bbc.co.uk/news/world-europe-64063047

34 https://www.bbc.co.uk/news/business-65313822

35 https://www.wired.co.uk/article/brexit-vote-whatsapp-groups

36 https://www.wired.com/story/whatsapp-facebook-data-share -notification/

37 https://www.qualtrics.com/news/qualtrics-announces-top-workplace
    -trends-to-watch-for-in-2022/
38 https://www.bloomberg.com/press-releases/2022-06-07/citrix-research
    -shows-hybrid-work-works
39 https://www.qualtrics.com/news/qualtrics-announces-top-workplace
    -trends-to-watch-for-in-2022/
40 https://www.wired.com/2002/06/spielberg/

Chapter 9: Are you standing still?

1   https://www.standard.co.uk/business/business-news/large-firms
    -lacking-board-level-diversity-risk-toxic-cultures-group-warns
    -b1087933.html
2   https://www.theguardian.com/football/2023/aug/21/luis-rubiales-kiss
    -outrage-spanish-football-fa-president-womens-world-cup-final-spain
    -jenni-hermoso
3   https://english.elpais.com/sports/2023-08-22/spains-acting-prime
    -minister-criticizes-federation-head-for-kissing-player-from-world
    -cup-champs.html
4   https://twitter.com/IreneMontero/status/1693345910112072129
5   https://sloanreview.mit.edu/article/the-toxic-culture-gap-shows
    -companies-are-failing-women/
6   https://en.wikipedia.org/wiki/Forever_21
7   https://www.bbc.com/news/business-49098060
8   https://assets.kpmg/content/dam/kpmg/xx/pdf/2022/09/kpmg-global
    -tech-report-2022.pdf
9   https://www.mckinsey.com/industries/public-and-social-sector/our
    -insights/government-transformations-in-times-of-extraordinary
    -change-key-considerations-for-public-sector-leaders
10 https://www.capgemini.com/resources/understanding-digital-mastery
    -today/
11 https://corpgov.law.harvard.edu/2020/01/13/corporate-culture
    -evidence-from-the-field/
12 https://psychology.illinoisstate.edu/ktschne/psy376/Hogan_Kaiser.pdf
13 https://joshbersin.com/wp-content/uploads/2021/10/BigReset_21_10
    -Deskless-Workers.pdf

14 https://www.cisco.com/c/m/en_us/solutions/global-hybrid-work-study.html

15 https://www.inc.com/marcel-schwantes/new-report-only-12-percent-of-employees-are-fully-productive-at-work-the-reasons-why-may-surprise-you.html

16 https://www.bloomberg.com/news/articles/2021-02-24/goldman-ceo-warns-remote-work-is-aberration-not-the-new-normal#xj4y7vzkg

17 https://www.cnn.com/2023/01/10/business/disney-return-to-work/index.html

18 https://nypost.com/2023/02/17/angry-disney-workers-warn-igers-return-to-office-plan-could-cause-long-term-harm/

19 https://www.wsj.com/articles/netflixs-reed-hastings-deems-remote-work-a-pure-negative-11599487219

20 https://www.washingtonpost.com/business/2018/07/18/open-office-plans-are-bad-you-thought/

21 https://knowledge.wharton.upenn.edu/article/how-companies-can-develop-anti-bias-strategies-that-work/

22 https://blog.google/technology/ai/ai-principles/

23 https://www.youtube.com/watch?v=p6PhtgiMYXw

24 https://www.theguardian.com/technology/2023/jul/11/ai-revolution-puts-skilled-jobs-at-highest-risk-oecd-says

25 https://www.key4biz.it/wp-content/uploads/2023/03/Global-Economics-Analyst_-The-Potentially-Large-Effects-of-Artificial-Intelligence-on-Economic-Growth-Briggs_Kodnani.pdf

26 https://www.washingtonpost.com/technology/2023/05/02/ai-jobs-takeover-ibm/?itid=lk_inline_manual_4

27 https://www.bloomberg.com/news/articles/2023-05-01/ibm-to-pause-hiring-for-back-office-jobs-that-ai-could-kill#xj4y7vzkg

28 https://twitter.com/totalvaligirl/status/1654004109991882752

29 https://www.theguardian.com/us-news/2023/may/26/hollywood-writers-strike-artificial-intelligence

30 http://www.mckinsey.com/global-themes/leadership/why-leadership-development-programs-fail

31 https://www.lifemeetswork.com/insights-archive/leading-intergenerational-workforce/

32 https://www2.deloitte.com/content/dam/Deloitte/global/Documents/HumanCapital/hc-2017-global-human-capital-trends-gx.pdf

33 https://www.mckinsey.de/~/media/McKinsey/Industries/Consumer%20Packaged%20Goods/Our%20Insights/Consumer%20organization%20and%20operating%20models%20Bold%20moves%20for%20the%20next%20normal/Consumer-organization-and-operating-models.pdf

Chapter 10: How will you respond?

1 https://assets.nationbuilder.com/plaid2016/pages/12287/attachments/original/1683121705/Prosiect_pawb_-_Key_findings_and_Summary_of_Recommendations_.pdf?1683121705

2 https://www.cnn.com/videos/politics/2018/09/18/anita-hill-1991-questioned-sexual-harassment-senate-orig-js.cnn

3 https://www.npr.org/2021/09/28/1040911313/anita-hill-belonging-sexual-harassment-conversation

4 https://www.archives.gov/milestone-documents/civil-rights-act

5 https://www.eeoc.gov/civil-rights-act-1991-original-text

6 https://www.upcounsel.com/civil-rights-act-of-1991

7 https://www.history.com/news/anita-hill-confirmation-hearings-impact

8 https://www.cbi.org.uk/media/m0pcest1/annex-to-open-letterapril23.pdf

9 https://www.ey.com/en_gl/risk/four-ways-boards-can-govern-culture-to-reduce-risk

10 https://www.herbertsmithfreehills.com/latest-thinking/the-new-world-of-work-report-warns-of-an-unprecedented-rise-in-workplace-activism-v2

11 https://www.ey.com/en_gl/risk/four-ways-boards-can-govern-culture-to-reduce-risk

12 https://www.politico.com/newsletters/women-rule/2022/03/11/the-woman-behind-the-gender-pay-gap-bot-00016526

13 https://www.frc.org.uk/getattachment/88bd8c45-50ea-4841-95b0-d2f4f48069a2/2018-UK-Corporate-Governance-Code-FINAL.pdf

14 https://www.auditboard.com/resources/ebook/cultivating-a-healthy-culture/

15 https://www.businessnewsdaily.com/10633-human-relations-movement.html

16 https://courses.lumenlearning.com/wm-introductiontobusiness/chapter/the-hawthorne-studies/ The Hawthorne Studies also introduced the world to the Hawthorne Effect, which is the change in behaviour by people in response to the knowledge that they are being observed.

17 https://www.emerald.com/insight/content/doi/10.1108/eb054960/full/html

18 http://www.hrmagazine.co.uk/article-details/glassdoor-trusted-more-than-employers

19 https://fortune.com/2022/07/19/glassdoor-court-order-reveal-employees-behind-anonymous-reviews/

20 https://scholar.google.com/scholar_case?case=303589675381977787&q=zuru+v+glassdoor&hl=en&scisbd=2&as_sdt=80000006

21 https://haskayne.ucalgary.ca/sites/default/files/teams/47/2022 per cent20Haskayne per cent20and per cent20Fox per cent20Accounting per cent20Conference/88_Paul per cent20Griffin_Does per cent20Free per cent20Speech per cent20Law.pdf

22 https://www.met.police.uk/police-forces/metropolitan-police/areas/about-us/about-the-met/bcr/baroness-casey-review/

23 https://www.reuters.com/article/india-education-tech-workers-idINL8N30Z4CC

24 https://www.dailyo.in/news/job-insecurity-false-promises-long-working-hours-why-byjus-work-culture-is-problematic-38288

25 https://www.theverge.com/2021/12/8/22823991/activision-blizzard-sexual-harassment-victim-press-conference

26 https://www.thegamer.com/activision-blizzard-breast-milk-stolen/

27 https://variety.com/2023/digital/news/activision-blizzard-ceo-addresses-toxic-workforce-claims-microsoft-deal-1235628361/

28 https://www.them.us/story/ellen-degeneres-show-faces-investigation-following-claims-of-toxic-work-environment

29 https://twitter.com/KevinTPorter/status/1241049881688412160?lang=en

30 https://www.hollywoodreporter.com/tv/tv-news/ellen-degeneres-addresses-workplace-allegations-changes-forthcoming-staff-letter-1305189/

31 https://variety.com/2020/tv/news/ellen-degeneres-sends-emotional
    -apology-to-staff-ep-ed-glavin-expected-to-depart-1234721495/
32 https://www.news.com.au/entertainment/tv/ellen-degeneres-sorry
    -letter-to-staff-slammed-as-worst-nonapology-ever/news-story/2d0
    df4d632c3e1f8ef76fc599148f0cd
33 https://www.latimes.com/entertainment-arts/tv/story/2020-09-21/ellen
    -degeneres-misconduct-allegations-apology-monologue
34 https://www.cbi.org.uk/media-centre/articles/open-letter-from-cbi
    -president-on-fox-williams-investigation/
35 https://www.sportengland.org/guidance-and-support/safeguarding/
    whyte-review
36 https://www.sportengland.org/guidance-and-support/safeguarding/
    whyte-review
37 https://www.theguardian.com/sport/2022/jun/16/british-gymnastics
    -report-anne-whyte-review-uk-sport-gymnasts-abused
38 https://www.linkedin.com/in/crisisandcomms/
39 https://www.fwc.gov.au/

Chapter 11: What to do if you work in a toxic culture now

1 https://mashable.com/article/ashley-judd-harvey-weinstein-lawsuit

Index